YES, THEY CAN!

YES, THEY CAN!

**A Practical Guide for Teaching
the Adolescent Slower Learner**

KENNETH J. WEBER
Faculty of Education
University of Toronto

METHUEN PUBLICATIONS
Toronto

McDOUGAL, LITTELL & COMPANY
Evanston, Illinois

Library of Congress
Catalogue Card Number
73-91770

ISBN
0 458 91030 9

Printed and bound in Canada

1 2 3 4 5 6   AP-74   9 8 7 6 5 4

Contents

Dedication

One of the great truths of publishing is that no one ever reads a dedication page — except perhaps those who may be included in it. Ironically, it is an almost absolute certainty that those who most deserve my gratitude will never read this: namely, the many adolescent slower learners I have met over years of teaching.

But to some who have helped me I can say thanks and know they will receive it: to Larry Darby, Dina Fayerman, Sheena Paterson, Nancy Young, Jim Foley, Carol Lyne and Bill LaCroix for their help and suggestions. I am grateful to other teachers of the adolescent slower learner whose work has given me both inspiration and ideas: Denis Stott, Daniel Fader, Brian Powell, David Holbrook and Neil Postman. Gail Murray's typing skills created a respectable-looking manuscript out of a handwritten mess. Of course I thank my wife Rita whose critical perception has always been more penetrating than mine, and not least my children whose exuberant but steady din kept me hiding at my desk over two long, Canadian winters to finish the book.

Ken Weber
January, 1974

PART A

The Adolescent Slower Learner
Who? ~ Why?
and
What To Do?

CHAPTER ONE

"We're the Dummies!"

The time: first day of a new school year; the scene: any classroom; the school: any school. The class is any group of adolescents — at least on the surface. But closer examination of the faces reveals that this group does not quite fit the stereotyped image of eager friendliness.

Some of the faces are rebellious; not the kind that is born of idealism, but the kind that is born of defeat and anger. Other faces reveal a brittle hardness, a kind of resentment. There is no wide-eyed wonder here.

Some of the faces are friendly; they show anticipation. But in the eyes there is an ever-so-subtle lurk of distrust. Scattered about are a few sad faces — sadness that grows from becoming old before their time. These faces have seen more of life by early adolescence than some people will ever experience, no matter how long they live. A few of the faces show the clear signs of bewilderment that develops from a handicap never diagnosed, or if diagnosed, not completely under control. Other faces betray nothing except a hint of vacuousness, a tired emptiness that comes from constant failure to cope with new situations.

The class is 9K or 10M, or Eighth Grade Opportunity Class, or First Year Remedial, or Grade Seven General Level, or Grade Nine Vocational, or Grade Eleven Phase One, or whatever euphemistic label the school system has chosen for its slower learners.

The door opens. A teacher enters. She is new, *obviously* new. There is a small, nervous smile. No response from the group. They've seen this before.

A pause while everyone waits for the ice to be broken.

"Good morning. My name is . . . . I'm your English teacher for this term. And you are — excuse me, is it 9M or 9N? There seems to be a mixup in my timetable."

"9M!"

"Yea 9M! You got it lady!"

"Hasn't the counsellor told you about us yet?"

"We're the special ones!"

"Yea! We're the dummies!"

A rather disheartening scenario. But one that is acted out every year in classrooms all over the world. It is an event that happens at least once in the career of every teacher. Unfortunately, it is a frequent event in the lives of these students, for it is the phrase, "We're the dummies!"

that reveals the overwhelming problem of adolescent slower learners. The one feature they all share is this utterly negative view of self; they lack, almost entirely, a sense of *self-worth*.

By the time a slower learner reaches his early or middle teens, he has usually acquired a history of failure that traces back to primary grades — even kindergarten or infant school. As is often the case, the failures are genuine. For one reason or another the student has not assimilated a certain body of knowledge, he has not developed a particular skill or has simply not been able to complete certain requirements. The cause may be one of many: an undiscovered physical handicap or other congenital defect; a disruptive home situation; intense sibling rivalry; a serious emotional conflict with a teacher in the very early years; intellectual lethargy. But whatever the cause, the sad fact is that by adolescence the slower learner has become accustomed to failure. In fact, he *expects* to fail.

The Failure Cycle And Its Results

This expectation of failure is part of a vicious circle. Because he perceives himself as a failure, the adolescent slower learner does not try hard; he makes no effort to learn on the theory that he "can't do it anyway". The frequent result is that he *does not,* in fact, *learn,* and when traditional-style tests are given to him, he fails yet again. Thus his initial perception of self is reinforced and the circle starts all over again. And each time, the circumference is smaller.

This attitude affects every aspect of the slower learner's education. Because he expects to fail, he often becomes rebellious and aggressive, avenging himself on a system he cannot conquer any other way. His energy is directed to defence rather than exploration. Other slower learners simply retreat, become morose, brooding and silent. Still others become dangerously explosive. Aware of their position, yet frustrated because they cannot cope with and overcome it, they are constantly hostile, simmering under the surface.

Some slower learners become entirely blasé about their situation. "We don't read," they will inform a new teacher. Not "We *can't* read," or "We *won't* read," but "We *don't* read." They are not apologizing; nor are they complaining. They are not even expressing defiance. They are simply saying to the new teacher: "This-is-where-we-are-and-now-that-you-know-don't-expect-anything-of-us-and-now-what-are-you-going-to-do?"

On the other hand, there are slower learning adolescents who react quite differently. They are aware that they may never match many of their peers. They believe they are in a special class for their own benefit. They try extremely hard, study and work, fret and worry about a *mere passing grade* with the same fervor that the scholarship class strives for perfection. When they fail, their disappointment is keen — but they are not surprised. And all too frequently the next effort they make is less intense. Success becomes progressively more elusive, and increasingly less worth the effort.

The Special Factor of Adolescence
In analyzing the characteristics of the adolescent slower learner, the overwhelming consideration must be the simple fact of their adolescence. There are the usual factors of the adolescent stage of life to consider, but adolescence becomes important in yet another sense: for whatever reasons the student is a slower learner, be they social, congenital, environmental, they are compounded by the fact that he has lived with them for quite some time. Whatever is "wrong" with the student has usually been wrong with him for a number of years. He not only suffers directly from the problems he may have, but he suffers indirectly from the fact of living with them for a long period of time. What most teachers face, therefore, are students who may well be slower learners, for one reason or another, but who by adolescence have become so accustomed to their state that their attitude and their outlook on life overlap and in many cases even *obscure* the basic problem.

From the pedagogical viewpoint then, the teacher's first task is to deal with this problem of attitude. Even though the teacher may have at hand, all the available background information on the student, all the available gimmickry, all the effective materials, the first step in teaching him is, in a sense, *de-conditioning*: to replace the syndrome of "if-at-first-you-don't-succeed-give-up" with one of "Yes, I can!" This is so because no matter what kind of corrective, or remedial, or therapeutic program a teacher may attempt, it will have very little lasting effect without the cooperation of the student. The student must feel that he has a *chance,* that he can do things well, and that he has as much to contribute to the world, in his own way, as any other person. He must be led to discover the unique value of his own thinking. Only then will the student "learn", or the teacher "teach".

As For This Book
The following chapters don't pretend that failure can be eliminated. Regrettably, the fact of failure is part of living and ignoring such reality is reserved for philosophers and some officials in education. What *can* be eliminated, however, is *defeat,* the overwhelming hopelessness and despair that school teaches so many slower learners.

In the pages that follow, the basic premise is one of teaching for success. The two sections that follow immediately, expand a definition of the slower learner, and recommend a style of curriculum. The largest part of the book outlines a series of practical approaches geared to the needs, psychological and practical, of the adolescent slower learner.

CHAPTER TWO

"Who Are the Students in a Class of Adolescent Slower Learners?"

The above is an unwieldly chapter title to be sure, but a necessary one nevertheless. It would have been easier to ask: *"Who* are the slower learners?" or even *"What* is a slower learner?" A response to either of these questions could then be found in a literal interpretation of the term, i.e., a student who lacks intellectual capacity. A response could also be found in an administrative interpretation — a student who does not meet the standards set by a school system. Unfortunately, neither definition would reflect with accuracy, the reality of the classroom.

This reality, as any teacher of the adolescent slower learner will attest, is one which goes much deeper than the fact of intellectual capacity. Students in these classes are placed there for a host of reasons. Some are there because they *apparently* lack intellectual capacity. Others have a physical handicap serious enough to retard their progress, but not serious enough to warrant special, individualized treatment. The adolescent slower learner class usually has a share of psychologically disturbed students; a sampling small or large, of students who have been unable to adjust to a new language; and of course, a number of "behavior problems" who have been assigned to the class for lack of a better solution. Most of them, according to rigidly-timed, mass-group tests, "can't read" or "demonstrate a need for remedial work". And all of them, each with his or her own *individual* problem, have been lumped together into one class.

Some Typical Cases

The following case studies are real ones. Each of them describes a student from 9F, a typical class of adolescent slower learners. Every experienced teacher of this kind of student has similar case studies, whether written, or stored in memory. These are a few of mine.

> Paul, aged 15. Fourth of six children, both parents living. Paul was born in a remote fishing village on the northeast coast of New-foundland. His parents moved to Toronto when he was 9. His father, after years of unemployment because of the deteriorating state of the fishing industry, moved to find work. He is presently working in a car wash.
>
> Paul has two outstanding characteristics. He is pleasant, happy, always smiling; and he is very, very slow-moving. Paul *never* finishes work at the same time as the rest of the class. He never arrives on time, and is always the last to leave. Paul's response to

any stimulus is a huge, unstinting grin. Interviews with former teachers lead me to suspect that he subconsciously discovered early in life that his disarming smile was an effective avoidance technique. He accomplished by grinning what others had to do by working or responding. And no one it seems, ever persisted in an attempt to break the pattern. On the Wechsler Intelligence Scale for Children, Paul tested at 74.2 for Verbal I.Q. and at 80.1 for Performance I.Q. I cannot believe that any test with a time limit could be even remotely accurate in Paul's case.

Because he never manages to complete anything, and because he constantly misplaces whatever work he does finish, Paul's achievement record is poor. Yet, though he is supposed to be a non-reader, he read a short story about two boys lost on a fishing dory with enthusiasm. He followed this immediately by reading two novels I gave him — both on nautical subjects.

Paul is a perfect example of the kind of student who because of simple lethargy, physical or intellectual, just does not keep up. He has been relegated to the slower learner class, not because he necessarily lacks intelligence, but because he cannot keep pace with the style of learning his culture demands. By age 15, Paul has developed a standard pattern of behavior. After discovering the effect of his grin, coupled with his easy-going personality, he was probably able to submerge himself in a class where more insistent, demanding students captured the teacher's attention. By mid-adolescence Paul's "being behind" was assured. And if there were any doubts, a *timed* intelligence test was the final blow.

Paul, like many of his slower learning colleagues, is a victim of pace. This in itself would not be so serious, except that both Paul and his teachers believe he is stupid, and both adjust themselves to that belief, rather than to the problem of pace.

Mark, aged 14. Living with his mother. Father abandoned family when Mark was 3. Has two older brothers. Mother has worked as a cleaning lady for 12 years.

Mark is black. He is sullen, brooding, explosive — and bright. He can write extremely well and sensitively — but won't. He refuses to read. His vocabulary is excellent, but he *deliberately* speaks a combination of pidgin and street slang. There are no Wechsler results for him because he refused to answer questions when it was administered. He never brings a book; never has writing materials. He sits in class and does nothing. Other students leave him entirely alone, or treat him with great respect.

His file reveals six suspensions for deliberately breaking windows, fighting, writing obscenities on the walls, suspected marijuana peddling, etc. He was assigned to this class with the admonition to me, "There's nothing you can do. Just try to make him behave."

Although Mark's teachers are genuinely afraid of him, he has done nothing for over a year to warrant such fear.

Like Paul in the previous case, Mark is almost a stereotype: the "discipline case". Often, this type of student is placed in a slower learner group out of desperation on the part of school officials. It is felt, they say, that he can do less damage — to himself and others — in such a class. His disruptive effects will be minimized because a slower learner class: (a) is noisy and undisciplined to begin with; (b) studies less important material and therefore can afford to absorb one more problem. Sometimes whole classes are composed of students like Mark.

The presence of Mark and those like him in a slower learner class has two results. The most obvious is that the unacceptable behavior usually continues. Less obvious is the fact that Mark's ability goes untouched and undeveloped. His achievement, more likely his *desire* to achieve, diminishes even further. He becomes bored and the unacceptable behavior intensifies. It takes only two or three Marks in one slower learner class to give the whole group an unfavorable reputation.

Linda, aged 13. Both parents living. Father is a successful accountant. She is the fifth of six children. Linda is an epileptic. Suffers from *grand mal* seizures. The attacks are controlled by strong depressant drugs, so strong that she is constantly depressed, breaks into tears at any time for no apparent reason.

Linda cannot work for more than five to ten minutes at once. After each short span of activity, she sits and stares sadly at nothing, as though looking further into her own soul for the cause of such sorrow. This habit, of course, has affected her productivity. The Wechsler Test gave her 69.7 for Verbal I.Q. and 76.2 I.Q. for Performance, but I suspect such low results are owing to her failure to work continuously.

Linda's most urgent problem (i.e. non-medical problem) is her perception of herself. The five siblings are all successful academic students and she feels she is a disgrace to the family. In our discussions she has mentioned suicide twice.

Linda has no friends. She talks to no one. She sits alone. She is the saddest child I have ever met.

There are Lindas in every class of adolescent slower learners: children who are not handicapped enough to receive highly specialized treatment, or children who suffer from handicaps for which the educational system has no remedy.

9

Most students with handicaps have suffered from them since birth and thus have usually begun their schooling just slightly less well-equipped than their peers. Each year, the gap widens so that by adolescence they are "behind". In addition of course, there is the old problem of self-perception. Some handicapped students are overly aggressive in their attempts to compensate. Some hide behind their handicap. Others trade on it. But most of them share one common feature: they are not quite capable of normal physical function, yet they are not sufficiently extreme cases of their type to warrant schooling which caters exclusively to their problems. Hence, they are placed in slower learner classes regardless of their ability. The stutterers, the partially deaf, the ones with slight defects, the obese, the epileptics — all these people have ability. It may be of a different nature; it may be harder to develop. But so often it goes undiscovered because so much time is spent in remediation. So much effort goes into *making them normal,* that any real talents they have, are rarely put to use. And of course, ignored in the process are the over-riding psychological factors which have developed over years of living with the handicap.

> Andrew, aged 12. Elder of two boys. Father a labourer. Mother an invalid. Andrew has a part-time job to help support the family. He doesn't sleep in class, but the job saps his energy.
>
> Practicality is Andrew's philosophy. He devotes great effort to his technical subject (carpentry), tolerates English because it has reading and writing skills, but endures his other subjects only with great reluctance. Unless there is practical value — *immediate* practical value — in a task, Andrew dismisses it.
>
> He dismisses abstract reasoning, conjecture, and imagination as a waste of time. Yet apparently in carpentry, his designs, and his solutions to building modification problems are superb. Although he scored only 86.1 for Performance I.Q. on the Wechsler Scale, he scored higher on one of my creative problem solving tests than any member of an experimental group of university graduates.
>
> A note in Andrew's personal file states that he has "a different kind" of intelligence.

Is intelligence absolute? Or does one need a certain "kind" of intelligence to succeed in school? Is the intelligence that interprets literature, different from the intelligence that designs and builds a circular staircase? If there *is* a difference, then is the first kind *better* than the second? Students think so, especially those in slower learner classes. In fact, many students do not usually regard the second kind as intelligence at all. And the education system does little to discourage this thinking.

There are many Andrews in a slower learner class — many students who do not see value in academic pursuit. And there are variations on the Andrew theme, too, like those students who reject academic pursuit because of family or cultural conditioning. ("School is the place where you learn a trade and get a job so don't waste your time on silly frills".)

Whatever the reason, Andrew and his colleagues do not accept, and hence do not adopt the world of the academic subject teacher. As a result, they do not perform well, and as often as not are regarded as simply *slow*.

> Antonina, aged 14. Both parents alive. Both work. Third of eight children. Entire family arrived from Portugal four years ago. All ten live in the same house with another family of seven.
>
> Antonina is a victim of culture-shock. Her family, of Portugese peasant stock, maintains the old ways. Antonina was betrothed at age 4, to a boy who still lives in Portugal. She awaits his coming with anticipation, and fear. To anticipate marriage is honorable, and it makes her popular with other girls in the class. Yet she would rather date, or go to parties, or even go out after dark. Her desire to break out of the traditional role for peasant women leads to terrible fights with her family.
>
> Antonina's other difficulty is with the language. She speaks with an accent, has great difficulty with English sentence structure, although her reading is surprisingly good. However, her father took exception to a romantically designed cover on a novel she was given in my class. The parish priest must now censor all her reading. (He's cooperative.)
>
> Although she confines her discussion and writing to marriage and romance, Antonina is surprisingly perceptive. She rarely pursues a topic very far however, because such contemplation or deep analysis is not, she feels, within the role of women. Thus, despite the conflict with her parents, to a great extent she has already internalized the traditional female, peasant role of her native country.

How many Antoninas must there be in slower learner classes! To change countries — to change *cultures* — in adolescence, must be a searing shock to the psyche. Antonina, like so many of her colleagues, comes to a new country when she is too old to learn the new culture in a natural way, as children do, and too young to have absorbed sufficient of her parents' culture to meet securely, the impact of the new one. She is, literally, in a cultural no-man's land. And like Andrew she is unable — and probably unwilling — to adopt her teachers' culture. The result? She is placed in a slower learner class.

The problem presented by Antonina's case is often magnified by the fact that, in large urban areas especially, whole classes, even whole schools are made up of students like her. And they are usually treated as slower learners for two reasons. In the first place, the local school system may have an *initial* program for immigrant students when they first arrive in the country, but it usually *does not* have a transitional program designed to help the students make the leap from acclimatization to participation. Secondly, the vast majority of teachers are simply not trained to deal with this type of student. Consequently, the only option seems to be to place Antonina in a slower learner class. She may in fact be slower than students in the regular program, but her slowness is not necessarily owing to an intellectual gap, but more likely to a cultural, linguistic one.

> Debbie, aged 16. Lives with her mother. Father in prison on seventh assault charge. She is eldest of three.
> Debbie's physical appearance telegraphs her attitude and personality. She could be very attractive, but wears heavy red lipstick and thick makeup. Her eyes are watery, a trifle bloodshot and *hard*. She has a brassy voice, a brassy laugh, and a rude, sharp tongue. Debbie flaunts herself openly, and brags loudly about her night-time exploits, and her activities in the drug culture. Her whole attitude toward school, toward teachers — toward any authority, is *defiance*. In class she blurts out responses, makes *sotto voce* comments to her friends, and tortures the younger, more immature boys in the class. She is such a dominant force that her moods can literally change the atmosphere of the whole class.
> Debbie is quick-witted, has an excellent memory, a vivid imagination. She calls herself stupid, yet is clearly aware that she is not. Her bitterness is almost overwhelming. She tested at an average of only 94.1 on the Wechsler Scale. Without doubt, an invalid result.
> I was able to learn from her, what I think is the reason for this low figure. Among her father's other problems, he was an alcoholic. One of his regular "games" was to threaten Debbie's mother with a knife and make the children watch. It was the morning after one of these episodes that Debbie wrote the test!

The presence of Debbies in adolescent slower learner classes, requires little comment. Most teachers would recognize the type, and most would acknowledge Debbie's latent ability. Yet few would find her easy to tolerate, for she is the type of student who singlehandedly, can create an unfavorable reputation for a whole class.

There is little doubt that by age 16, Debbie is a slower learner, at least in education's customary terms. She has built such a shell around herself, and has spent so much time lashing out at a system she hates, that by this time, she is genuinely "behind". And no one is likely to penetrate Debbie's shell by pedagogical means, or by choice and style of curriculum. The only way to help Debbie is on a human-to-human basis. But the average teacher faces so many other insistent demands, all of which must be met in the midst of Debbie's disruption, that to reject rather than help her seems a very natural and honest reaction.

> Gary, aged 12. Both parents living. One older brother. His father is a lawyer.
> Gary is the class fool. The jester. His short, stocky body, his wide mouth and slight acne have given him a cruel nickname: "The Toad". But Gary revels in it; in fact he promotes it.
> His behavior is never malicious but always disruptive. He will work but only with my personal encouragement. He is terribly insecure. When he succeeds at something — which is not infrequent — he is always very surprised.
> The source of Gary's difficulties seems easy to understand. His father will have nothing to do with him, and openly refers to Gary — in comparison with his older son — as "stupid". Gary's older brother has constantly won top honors as a scholar; he is a student leader and a community organizer.
> At school, and at home, Gary became a victim of his older brother's record. Both his parents, and apparently his teachers as well, challenged Gary by comparing his performance with that of his older brother. Gary couldn't meet the challenge.
> A very interesting set of Wechsler results — if they're worth anything — is: Verbal Aptitude 114.2 and Performance Aptitude 89.3.

No one really knows whether Gary is a slower learner — not even Gary. Throughout his school career, he has so studiously avoided doing anything which might invite comparison with his older brother that it is impossible to tell what, if any, talent he has. Certainly, like many other slower learners at the adolescent stage, he is "behind". And like many others, he is a bit of a "problem"; the class fool always is.

Fortunately for most teachers there is usually only one Gary in a class. But the factor that helped to make Gary a slower learner is far more common. Fear of failure, fear of comparison, fear of ridicule — these are fears which create candidates for a slower learner class. And the fear operates in several ways. There are students who allow themselves to settle into a slower learner class in a very conscious way; they *want* to be where the work is easier. For others, fear makes them avoid challenge subconsciously, so that their placement in the slower learner class becomes necessary because of non-achievement, or non-effort. And of course, there is the old problem of those who fear timed, standardized tests. As a result, they usually score low, contributing yet another unfavorable statistic to their personal files.

Sharon, aged 15. A ward of the state. She has never been adopted, and no foster home has kept her for more than two years. Our school is her eighth.

Sharon is short, fat, very plain, and constantly exudes body odour. Her peers avoid her, and her teachers find it very difficult to care for her.

Unlike some adolescents who compensate for an unattractive appearance with an attractive personality, Sharon has set up a series of defences which match her physical appearance. Her attitude and her tongue are so vicious that none of her peers — not even Debbie — dare cross her path. With adults she fabricates long, involved stories of her achievements.

She has been in juvenile court once, charged with cruelty to animals, and she's been arraigned twice for possession of marijuana.

Interestingly, her Wechsler result for Verbal Aptitude was only 91.0. Yet I have personally given her over twenty novels — all happy-ending romances — so far this year, and I'm convinced she's read and understood them. She has read nothing, however, for the last three weeks. Apparently she had entertained high hopes of being adopted by her present foster parents, but learned recently that her hopes were in vain. Because she is fifteen this was probably her last chance.

What does a teacher do with Sharon? Physically unattractive, socially maladjusted, unfriendly, unhappy, Sharon presents a terribly difficult problem to any school system. There is probably no doubt that she belongs in the adolescent slower learner class. There has never been any continuity in her life, no thread of security at home or at school; she has had no one to relate to. Is it any wonder that Sharon is "behind"?

But the case of Sharon and her stereotype casts the average slower learner *curriculum* into a sharp perspective. Is it likely that someone with Sharon's outlook would be concerned about bare subjects and bare predicates? Would such knowledge give her the kind of help she needs? Would Sharon be helped by exercises which underline the correct word? Or what would she gain from "home management" courses so often taught to adolescent girls in slower learner classes?

The case of Sharon forces a teacher to ask the question that should be asked every day: "Exactly what are the *needs* of the adolescent slower learner, and what am I doing to meet them?"

Who Are the Slower Learners?

The previous case studies presented a broad array of "typical" adolescent slower learners and most experienced teachers would recognize many of their own students, wholly or in part, in each of these studies. But the list of typical cases could be expanded ad infinitum, with every teacher adding yet another variety, yet another kind of slower learner. To reach any simple conclusion about the specific nature of the slower learning adolescent is of course, very difficult. This is particularly so in view of the fact that each slower learner class presents a different reality. A class will be different, depending on the number of Debbies or Marks, or Andrews or Antoninas. A class will be different because of particular school policy. A class is different because of its racial or ethnic composition, or different because of the teachers with whom it must relate. There is no one kind of adolescent slower learner, and no one kind of adolescent slower learner class. In short, a definition of the adolescent slower learner — in real terms — is impossible.

What can be advanced however, are a few observations that may help to isolate the situation to a degree where some of the needs might be analyzed.

1. The only feature shared in common by all members of a class of adolescent slower learners is an utter lack of confidence and self-respect. They have little or none of the sense of self-worth that motivates Western man.

2. "Lacking in intelligence" is an inadequate and inaccurate means of defining adolescent slower learners, and timed, standardized intelligence or achievement tests are not a reliable indicator of their true ability.

3. The immediate needs of these students are often as much *social* and *emotional,* as intellectual, and in many cases, attempts at fulfilling intellectual needs without first recognizing the others, are utterly futile.

4. The social, the cultural, the behavioral — the entire *life-outlook* of an adolescent slower learner is likely to be quite different from that of his teachers.

5. As a final observation, the following survey results offer what is quite likely another common feature of students in a class of adolescent slower learners.

Although its statistics speak loudly for themselves, the terminology of the following table requires a bit of explanation. In 1960, Canada's most populous province, Ontario, initiated a plan which was theoretically designed to create programs tailored to the ability of every student eligible for secondary school.* On the table, there are four such programs.

---

* The program was drastically revised in 1972.

The "5 year" was a normal university-bound program; the type that, traditionally, has always existed.

There followed, three different types of slower learner programs. The "4 year" was for reasonably capable students. It was oriented toward technical subjects, and theoretically led to admission into a polytechnical institute.

The "2 and 3 year" program was designed for students of less ability. It was very vocationally oriented, toward such trades as auto mechanics, horticulture, etc.

The "Special Vocational" program was as its name implies, almost exclusively vocational. It was designed for those students who had demonstrated the least intellectual ability and interest.

In 1970, the Board of Education for the City of Toronto published the results of a survey taken of all its students in secondary schools. For teachers of the adolescent slower learner, the interesting observations are these: *Note the relationship between the occupation of the head of household, and the proportion of students in the slower learner programs; compare the figures for such occupations as #9 and #13, or #8 and #2,* and ask again: Who are the students in a class of adolescent slower learners?

Programs Attended by Secondary School Students
(Categorized by occupation of head of household)

		Secondary School Program				
Occupation	N	Special Voca-tional %	2 & 3 Year %	4 Year %	5 Year %	Total %
2 - laborers, taxi drivers, etc.	11399	9.0	12.8	31.7	46.5	100.0
3 - sheetmetal workers, mechanics, etc.	2312	6.5	8.7	29.4	55.5	100.1
4 - sales clerks, machinists, etc.	1693	5.4	6.6	27.6	60.4	100.0
5 - printing workers, electricians, etc.	3060	3.8	6.4	28.7	61.1	100.0
6 - dental technicians, embalmers, etc.	2311	3.2	4.9	23.7	68.2	100.0
7 - musicians, athletes, etc.	1496	1.2	3.2	21.6	74.1	100.1
8 - clergymen, librarians, etc.	1661	1.9	3.4	17.1	77.7	100.1
9 - accountants, engineers, lawyers, etc.	2609	.5	1.2	8.7	89.7	100.1
10 - retired, Workman's Compensation	445	5.8	4.7	28.5	60.9	99.9
11 - Welfare, Mother's Allowance	98	28.6	24.5	25.5	21.4	100.0
12 - university student, adult retraining	96	5.2	10.4	25.0	59.4	100.0
13 - unemployed	801	22.1	13.1	29.1	35.7	100.0
14 - housewife	1451	13.6	15.5	32.2	38.7	100.0
15 - student on his own	60	—	5.0	33.3	61.7	100.0
TOTAL	30624*	6.6	8.9	26.9	57.7	100.1

* No information for 1132 students.

E. N. Wright, *Student's Background and its Relationship to Class and Program in School (The Every Student Survey)*. Toronto: The Board of Education for the City of Toronto, Research Department, 1970 (#91), p. 37.

CHAPTER THREE

"Keep Them Busy — and Never Turn Your Back!"

Adolescent slower learners are often difficult to teach — or at least different from what most teachers are accustomed to. These students, it seems, will not or do not know how to "play school" in the way that guarantees success. Their behavior is frequently in direct conflict with their teachers' wishes; unlike "normal" students, they do not accept without question the pre-packaged curricula which someone else has decided for them, and again unlike their "normal" peers, they do not see any value in pursuing the goals which the world of education holds before them.

Because adolescent slower learners are different in this way, an entire body of mythology has developed around them — a whole catalogue of half-truths, misconceptions, and confusions leading right from the simple fact of terminology up to the more complex problems of methodology and program. What follows here, is a brief summary of the more outstanding of these myths.

Myth #1:
Terminology

Generally, educators tend to use terms in the same way a drunkard uses a lampost: for support rather than for illumination. The terminology we use to describe adolescent slower learners tends to be so absolute, so final, and so damning, that it not only denies any possibility of hope, but justifies the negative attitude and treatment these students so often endure. For example, consider the description, *terminal,* a still-popular phrase in North America. It is a term, as many people have pointed out, from the death-vocabulary of medicine. Think of what it must mean to know you are a *terminal student.* What is a teacher's attitude, knowing that he is teaching *terminal* students? Or consider the equivalent in England: *educationally sub-normal* (the E.S.N. student). Like *terminal, educationally sub-normal* is no longer an official term, but it is still widely used. And in effect, it is just as damaging.

Consider another term, primarily American: the *disadvantaged.* It is particularly suited to the American dream that anyone can be President because *disadvantaged* implies economic, or cultural, or environmental deprivation. All an education system needs do is engineer change in the situation, and the "disadvantaged" student will gain all the benefits that white middle-class culture has to offer.

Some labels have no implication at all. They are simply blunt: the *slow* learner, used particularly in North America, and the *backward* child, still in use in England.

Less damning, but at best confusing are terms so broad in scope that they are meaningless: perceptually handicapped, dyslexic, learning disabled. Unfortunately, these terms become labels in the minds of their chief users (all too frequently those people who don't quite understand what they mean). And once a child is thus labelled, his chances for real help diminish quickly.

Terms and labels are a serious problem in dealing with the adolescent slower learner because they encourage teachers and administrators to identify these students — consciously and otherwise — in a disparaging way. Our terminology is so easy to hide behind, so easy to use when excusing ourselves. Granted, something like *terminal* is more administrative than pedagogical in intent, but it is a label which invites teachers to ignore potential ability; it is a label which underlines for a teacher the fact that here is a student who is never going on to study the great things *he* did at university. Even worse, the student is also aware of his label, so that even before they meet, he and his teacher are "ready" for each other.

A Small Plea for The Slower Learner

Because teacher and student expectation is so strongly affected by terminology, it might seem wise to abandon it altogether. More palatable perhaps might be the adoption of terminology which accepts a reality without making that reality a condemnation. A slow*er* learner is often behind his colleagues on the educational achievement scale, but this does not mean that he will never achieve. He may achieve in a different way, or it may take him longer. But to label him as simply *slow* is to do him an injustice, for his slowness is not absolute. He may just be slow in specific academic pursuits. Students with handicaps are usually slow*er* for obvious reasons, but they can and do succeed. The "discipline problem" students are slow*er* for yet other reasons.

Slower may not be an attractive term, but no useful term for these students can remain attractive for long. (Note what has happened to the term "approved school" in England, a term originally selected because it was so innocuous.) *Slower* is at least descriptive of a reality, and if nothing else, it is free of the taint of absoluteness. If a student is known as simply slow*er,* there can be less tendency to dismiss him, for the term does contain the implication that he can eventually succeed, maybe in a different way, maybe via a different route, but he *can* succeed!

19

Myth #2
Remediation

Reminiscences: My First Parent-Meets-Teacher Night

> Meeting Lazlo's father promised to be routine at first. The family had emigrated from Hungary only five years before. Lazlo's accent was still quite noticeable. His father's was thick, and he seemed reluctant to speak at all.
>
> Lazlo was in my tenth grade *remedial reading* class. We had a room called a reading "lab" (as though reading could be taught like urinalysis), an impressive array of machines (which neither I nor the students understood, but we played with them anyway) and an abundant supply of drill books.
>
> Lazlo's father was attentive as I explained all the wonderful things we were doing for his son. In fact I thought he was quite appreciative — until his first comment:
>
> "Can you sex chicks*?"
>
> My flabbergasted silence led him to repeat the question.
>
> "Can *you* sex chicks?"
>
> Only when I ventured a tentative, and uninformed, "No", did he follow through.
>
> "Well, you know, *I* can. And *Lazlo* can too! And do you know something? *We're not going to make you learn!*"
>
> With that, Lazlo's father turned to leave. But when he reached the door he paused for one final comment. Pointing a thick, stubby finger at me he said, without animosity, "That's the trouble with all you teachers; you buggers try to make everybody else just like yourselves!"

An interesting view of remediation. And maybe, just maybe, a very accurate one. What Lazlo's father said, put into a more philosophical idiom, is that remedial programs are a symptom of education's failure — or unwillingness — to recognize diversity. So many remedial programs, or as they are sometimes called, *compensatory* programs are primarily designed to direct the learner back into the main stream — or at least into the stream that society and education have conceived as main, namely, the primrose path to higher education. Remedial programs of this kind, it seems, cannot accept the student *as he is*. Rather than beginning with the student, and developing a program to suit his needs, remediation usually means fitting the student to the program.

Particularly with the adolescent, the concept of remediation is a potentially destructive one. Consider for example, an adolescent who is taking a remedial course in reading. (Usually he is *made* to take the

---

* Determine the sex of a chick at 4-6 days old.

20

course.) By adolescence he has developed a variety of defences, attitudes and modes of behavior toward reading, all of which tend to overlap and obscure the original reason for his "not being able to read", if indeed that really is the case. Yet what is customarily offered in most such courses are drills in comprehension, drills in vocabulary, drills in spelling. In other words, this student is given extra doses of what he has already demonstrated he cannot do in the first place. In addition — and much more serious — the apparent lack of reading ability, which in the case of most adolescents is a behavioral problem, is being treated exclusively as a skill. Because it approaches the student's reading problem simply as a skill, the remedial aspect therefore, has little transfer. Granted, the student may develop real skill within the confines of the remedial program; he may become a master at answering drills or following a light ray on a controlled reading machine. But unless his attitudes, his behavioral problems are taken care of, he will lapse right back into the same situation he was in before being enrolled in the remedial program.

So many people assume that if the *skill* of reading is taught — or re-taught — the behavioral aspect, the lack of *reading habit,* will correct itself willy-nilly. But for the adolescent, *remediation alone, is simply too late.* His needs at this stage are developmental ones. He must be developed as a whole person. Little can be done for him by singling out one flaw and working on it alone.

Myth #3:
Streaming (Ability Grouping)

It is unfortunate that the practice of grouping students according to their abilities — a generally beneficial advance in education — is somewhat of a mixed blessing for adolescent slower learners. On the one hand there is little doubt that streaming gives the slower learner the advantage of separation to permit adjusted programs. The special emphasis that he requires probably would not be possible in an unstreamed situation.

But it is a ridiculous notion to assume that a slower learner class, by its very nature, is made up of students of relatively homogeneous ability. In fact, the only common feature shared by the students of this class is a failure to cope with the regular system. Although they share the problem of *educational* disability, the reasons for it are so diverse, so distinct with each student, that to treat the class effectively as a single unit, is almost impossible. Yet most teachers are accustomed to teaching "the class", the whole unit at once. And this technique is usually successful with non-slower learning adolescents, because most classes of this type have at least a common denominator of ability — or willingness — from which to build. This is not usually true of a slower learner class, and it leads to frustration.

For example, English teachers who attempt to teach the same novel to an entire class at once — a time-honored procedure with regular classes — are often frustrated with slower learners, because rarely will the same novel appeal to the whole class. Frequently, the novel is too difficult for some in the class or too simple for others. Similar frustrations are felt by teachers in every discipline.

Streaming provides only a minor beginning for the adolescent slower learner; it simply creates a reasonably separate environment. But from this point, a teacher's planning must go further. A slower learner must somehow be able to enjoy the security of the class unit, the morale that grows from being a part of something; yet at the same time, if he is to learn at all, he must begin at that fine point where his interests and his abilities meet. In other words, a teacher of adolescent slower learners is faced with the awesome and paradoxical task of what might be called "collective individualization": the attempt to promote the idea of the *class,* the *unit* of which each student is a part, while at the same time allowing each student to progress at the style and pace best suited for him. Succeeding chapters of this book provide some suggestions for accomplishing this.

Myth #4:
"They're All Bad"

Reminiscences: Egon vs. the Substitute Teacher

> Teaching Egon would have been a learning experience for anyone. In my class, he was never openly malicious, and most of the time was too confused to be mischievous. His work was of fairly high calibre, but as the butt of so many practical jokes, he rarely had the chance to finish what he started.
>
> As far as his teachers were concerned, Egon had a two-sided problem. He stammered badly, and he swore fluently. The irony was that whenever he swore, his sentences flowed trippingly off the tongue. But without this linguistic aid, the stammer made most of his speech incomprehensible.
>
> In an uninformed, but mildly effective attempt to remedy the problem, we who taught Egon had begun a system of asking him only questions which could be answered in a single word without the need for a qualifying adjective.
>
> All was well until the day Egon's mathematics teacher became ill. Her substitute for the day was a retired teacher, a stout, fidgety, irritating woman who happened to be the wife of a local clergyman.

No one bothered to explain to her the case of Egon.

In the course of her lesson with his class she presented a problem in metrics.

"Now!" she gushed, "we know there are a thousand meters! And we know there are ten thousand centimeters! Now! How many milli-meters do you think there are, Egon?"

Egon tried his best.

"M-m-mu-mu-must be fuckin' near a million, ma'am!"

His answer got poor Egon a one-day suspension, and it led to a furor in the community over 'what-is-happening-in-that-school!'

Egon's case is an unfortunate but clear demonstration of one reason why the adolescent slower learner is tarred with the reputation of bad behavior. He ran directly into a situation of cultural conflict, and lost.

Like it or not, we teachers are victims of a "halo effect" which bedevils our judgment. We allow ourselves to be affected by factors which often have little to do with the case in point. How many of us are influenced in our judgment of a student's ability, by his appearance? or by his manners? or by his pattern of speech? And how strong is this influence in a slower learner class where the proportion of unkempt hair, faulty hygiene, misapplied cosmetics, and poor manners seems to be so much higher than in regular classes?

But the "halo effect" is still an oblique explanation of the slower learner's reputation for bad behavior. So is the factor of cultural difference. There is still the stark reality that an adolescent slower learner class is frequently difficult to manage. In some classes the atmosphere is so disruptive that it is impossible for any learning to take place at all. In others, a teacher might expend so much energy in simply gaining control, that there remains neither strength nor will to teach. Whence then, comes the myth? It comes from the belief that slower learners are *naturally* ill-behaved!

To many teachers it must seem so. But consider things from the students' point of view. Why should they cooperate for a system with which they cannot cope? By their adolescence, experience has provided ample demonstration that the system is not doing much for them. And a whole class of students with that attitude is bound to lead to disruption, if only because of peer group pressure.

The solution, if there really is one, seems to be to change the attitude, somehow making the students confident that not only can they cope with the system, but that the system itself has something to offer them. As always however, if the solution is to work, the fact of adolescence must be kept in the forefront. Adolescent slower learners with their years of negative experience do not give their trust lightly. To change their attitude requires time, patience, understanding, and a willingness to overlook social and behavioral aberrations.*

It also requires adaptation in the style of curriculum. Extra doses of old familiar material are not likely to strike a chord of response.

Myth #5:
Standardized Tests, Reading Machines, And Drill Books

Ask Yourself These.

Standardized Tests:

1. Have you examined carefully the results of standardized tests given to your slower learning students? (Include general achievement, I.Q., and reading.)

2. Did the results tell you anything you didn't already know or suspect?

3. After examining the results, have you been able to maintain an entirely objective opinion of certain students?

4. If the test results indicated that certain of your students might have problems, did they also tell *what* problems?

5. Were these results obtained within the last year? If not, do you consider them valid now?

6. Do you know whether the test given your students was the appropriate one at the time?

7. What do you know about tests and testing? (e.g. Do you know the differences between the Gates-McGinitie Reading Tests and the Nelson-Deny Reading Tests?)†

8. What is the attitude of your students toward writing such tests?

9. Do you believe that intelligence, or achievement, or reading ability can be rigidly timed?

---

* See Chapter Fifteen, "Managing the Adolescent Slower Learner Class".

† In a questionnaire once presented to a group of fifty-seven practicing teachers, I posed the following: "For adolescents between the ages of 13 to 15, from homes where the income is below the national average, which test do you feel would provide the most accurate indication of their true intelligence, The Stanford-Binet or The Wassermann?" (The Stanford-Binet is of course, a widely recognized intelligence test; The Wassermann is a test for syphilis.) Seventeen teachers admitted honestly that they knew nothing about either test. Twenty-five said they would use The Stanford-Binet. And fifteen teachers, or 26.4 per cent of the group, recommended The Wassermann!

10. Please read the following paragraph in 25 seconds or less.

> ... suppose we set up the hypothesis that there is no real difference between statistical measures, say arithmetic means, of a certain aspect of pupils such as intelligence in two distinct populations, for instance boys and girls. Such hypotheses, namely, that the true difference between two statistical measures based on complete populations is zero, are called *null hypotheses*. Yet we usually obtain a difference greater or less than zero. If the null hypothesis is borne out, then this difference will not be greater or less than zero by an amount which could not be due merely to the fluctuations of random sampling. If the null hypothesis is disproved, the difference based on random samples drawn from the population must be considered to indicate a real difference greater or less than zero in the population.

There is little doubt that you could *read* this paragraph — or at least you could decode it. Could you answer some multiple choice questions about it? Assuming that you could, does this mean you *understood* the paragraph? Assuming again that you could answer the questions, does this mean that your reading ability has been accurately tested?

11. How many of your slower learners are confronted by passages like the one above in reading tests — passages in which they have not even the remotest interest, or about which they have not the slightest understanding? Do such items test their reading ability in a valid way?

Reading Machines:
1. How would reading machines help *you* personally, improve your reading?
2. Can you state *precisely* in what way reading machines help slower learners to read?
3. How do machines help slower learners to enjoy reading?

Drill Books:
Drill books have some usefulness. For one thing, they can reinforce or give practice in certain skills and concepts; they can be used to free the teacher from tedious chores; and at times they can be used to provide solitary activities for those periods of quietness that slower learners often need.

But drill books have a weakness — not in themselves as much as in what they encourage:

Have you ever used drill books as an escape?

As a means to keep students busy and thus avoid having to teach them?

Myth #6:

Train Them For Employment

There is no more hypocritical premise in the entire educational process than the one which ordains that the slower learner, because he does not perform adequately in the time-honored way, should be *trained for employment*. A false value in our system implies that school and society can discharge their obligation by giving the student a skill. And it is this value that leads to the design of slower learner curricula in which skill training comes first, curricula in which the student is prepared to serve the needs of industry and the economy.

To have a skill, or a particular training, is, of course, a distinct advantage in life. But for educators to make the acquisition of a skill the driving purpose behind a slower learner's schooling is inconsistent with the supposed reasons for education. Such a philosophy produces subservient qualities in a person. It makes him conveniently non-questioning and receptive to orders. And this century has already provided several lessons in the results of such a philosophy.

Further, it is interesting to note just who in our society receives the emphasis in training-style education. The Toronto survey mentioned earlier (Wright, 1970, p. 17) revealed, for example, that 36% of the students in academic, geared-to-university secondary schools came from a background of poverty (i.e. the head of household is identified as retired, unemployed, a housewife, pensioned, or on welfare.) For the students in the city's vocational schools, the figure was 83%! With such an incredible differential it is hard not to look to the "train them" philosophy for the reason.

And how much good does training do? How much benefit comes from this arbitrary — and expensive — form of education? Although there are many surveys, two are worth quoting here. In 1965, a study by Eninger* of graduates of 4-year technical schools in the United States, found that *71.2 per cent* of the graduates were *not* working in the jobs for which they had been trained. In 1972, in a study of graduates of special high schools and vocational schools, Reich and Zeigler† found that excluding the Clerical and Sales job category,‡ *eighty-two per cent*

---

* M. C. Eninger, *The process and product of technical and industrial high school level: the products* (Pittsburgh, Penn.: American Institute For Research, September, 1965).

† C. M. Reich & S. Zeigler, *A Follow-Up Study of Special Vocational and Special High School Students* (Toronto: The Board of Education for the City of Toronto, Research Department (#102), 1972), p. 16.

‡ The Clerical and Sales job category traditionally employs high numbers, exclusive of the number trained.

were not working in jobs related to their training course work! See chart below.

Other revelations in this survey were equally shocking. At a time when the national average of unemployment in Canada was high (circa 5.5 to 6.0%) these graduates reported an unemployment rate as follows:

with housewives included as employed	
Vocational Schools	**Special High Schools**
Of those reporting, 21.5% of the males and 20.5% of the females were unemployed.	Of those reporting, 28.12% of the males and 13.73% of the females were unemployed.

To say the least, results like these cast doubt on the training philosophy. But does it mean that the teaching of skills should be abandoned? Does it mean that teachers of technical subjects are redundant? Not likely. For one thing because technical teachers often come from industry — from "outside" instead of from one side of the teacher's desk to the other — they usually have a firmer grip on the nature of things than do some of their more academic colleagues. And in their technical subjects the students gain as much, cognitively, perceptively — and therapeutically — as in any academic subject. But what must be recognized by all educators, is that slower learners cannot just be *trained*. There is more to education. There is more to living.

CHAPTER FOUR

"But What Are You Going to Do With Them?"

I Taught Them All
Naomi John White

I have taught in a high school for ten years. During that time I have given assignments, among others, to a murderer, an evangelist, a pugilist, a thief, and an imbecile.

The murderer was a quiet boy who sat on the front seat and regarded me with pale blue eyes; the evangelist, easily the most popular boy in the school, had the lead in the junior play; the pugilist lounged by the window and let loose at intervals a raucous laugh that startled even the geraniums; the thief was a gay-hearted Lothario with a song on his lips; and the imbecile a soft-eyed little animal seeking the shadows.

The murderer awaits death in the state penitentiary; the evangelist has lain a year now in the village churchyard; the pugilist lost an eye in a brawl in Hong Kong; the thief, by standing on tiptoe, can see the windows of my room from the county jail; and the once gentle-eyed moron beats his head against a padded wall in the state asylum.

All of these pupils once sat in my room, sat and looked at me gravely across worn brown desks. I must have been a great help to these pupils — I taught them the rhyming scheme of the Elizabethan sonnet and how to diagram a complex sentence.

Nothing is more disturbing to a teacher than the nagging doubt that what he is doing for his slower learners — or any students for that matter — may not be what they really need. And every thinking teacher experiences this doubt; every teacher who cares about more than just his own survival, continually goes through the self-imposed process of analyzing objectives, methods, and curricula.

For teachers of the adolescent slower learner, the end result is often exasperation. Honest analysis reveals all too frequently that objectives, methods and curricula are more suited to the demands of administration, the budget, and tradition, than to the students. For them, suitability tends to be more a matter of coincidence than of specific direction.

A Matter of Needs

If educators are going to "do anything" with adolescent slower learners, then what must be analyzed first are their needs, present and future. And what do we know — really know — about their needs? Specifically, very little. All we really know about the *present* needs of adolescent slower learners is that traditional styles of curriculum do not seem to be fulfilling, or in some cases even useful. And we know that many of these students tend to look upon the desire for academic achievement as part of another world, a world that is not theirs. We also know that an urgent present need for them is self-confidence — the capacity to look at a challenge and say, "Yes, I can!"

And for their future, what do we know? Again, specifically very little; but as adults we have had the advantage of experience; we do know that adolescent slower learners, like everyone else, can expect certain things of life. We know that they will have to *think,* that life will present them with situations in which they will have to perceive, calculate, weigh evidence, determine courses of action. We know also that they will be confronted with situations that will arouse emotion, that their capacity to *feel* will be stretched, shrunk, bent, and many times forced beyond reasonable limits. We know too that some of life's situations can be conquered only if the people facing them have enough self-esteem, enough belief in themselves. And finally, we know that like everyone else, slower learners will probably engage in some kind of work. The work may require a talent or a skill, or merely a positive attitude, but just as with the other certainties of life, the degree of specific preparation possible in school, is limited.

It follows then, that whatever schooling we design for the adolescent slower learner, it must aim at developing *life-competence;* not only social competence, or functional competence, but rather the competence to deal with life in all its phases and with all the variables it presents. And it must also aim at developing *employment-competence,* not just training, but rather the capacity to come to grips with and master an employment situation.

An Immodest Proposal

Translating these aims into immediate, practical, classroom terms then, means that the flow of teaching emphasis must be directed *at the student* more emphatically than is usually the case. For example, instead of teaching literature for its own sake, we must teach literature to make our slower learners think and feel. Instead of teaching *reading,* we have to teach our students to *read.* Instead of teaching *vocabulary,* we must teach our students to *express themselves.* In short, rather than orient our objectives, methods and curricula around the development of skills, let us orient them around the development of the students. Develop the students *first,* and they will be better able to learn any skills they need. Develop their confidence and they will develop social competence themselves. Encourage them to think, and they will solve their own problems.

29

Show them that feelings are natural, and they will better understand themselves.

Our objectives, methods and curricula must recognize the *adolescent fact* of the adolescent slower learner. Teaching the skill of reading is a waste of time for students who refuse to read, or who think they are non-readers, or who do anything to avoid reading. These are people who have had a "reading problem" for a long time, and the problem is now considerably more complex than just lack of skill. The same factor applies to students who supposedly cannot write, or speak, or think, or feel. Only by dealing with the students first — their attitudes, their perceptions, their fears, their reluctance — can we teachers hope to accomplish anything. For unless our students participate actively in their own education, we are wasting our time — and theirs.

PART B

Practical Classroom Techniques

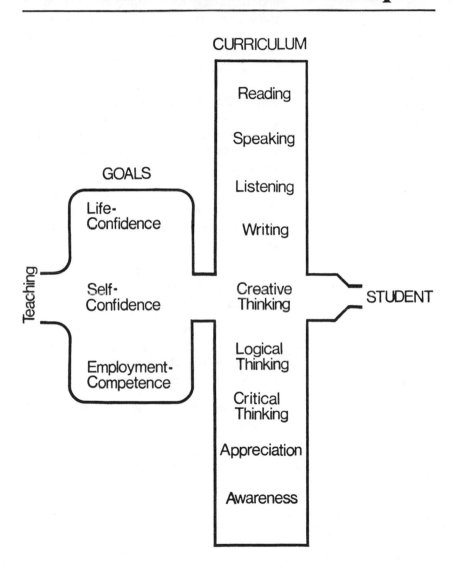

CURRICULUM

Reading

Speaking

Listening

Writing

GOALS

Life-
Confidence

Creative
Thinking

STUDENT

Teaching

Self-
Confidence

Logical
Thinking

Employment-
Competence

Critical
Thinking

Appreciation

Awareness

WHAT PART B IS ALL ABOUT

The practical techniques and suggestions that follow in Part B are based on realism — the realism of the classroom, where weak budgets, overcrowding, lack of materials, and other day-to-day problems can make lofty objectives seem painfully remote. Nevertheless, these techniques and suggestions aim at fulfilling the apparent needs of the adolescent slower learner. Above all, there are five principles to which the contents of Part B adhere strictly:

1. *Any* teacher can put these techniques into practice. None of them depends upon a particular kind of teaching personality.

2. Each technique is culturally immune. A student does not have to adopt the teacher's or the system's values and beliefs to learn. He can be what he is, and still develop.

3. Because they attempt to reach the adolescent slower learner *behaviorally,* the techniques encourage self-starting.

4. Flexibility must be built in; the need to approach a slower learning class with the realization that abilities will vary widely is a major part of each suggestion.

5. No technique requires vast sums of money.

CHAPTER FIVE

A Writing Program
for the Adolescent Slower Learner

Writing Program: Need #1
In any class of adolescent slower learners each student's writing must necessarily be approached individually and developed from the level at which he now works.

The following was written by a slower learner.

The Bus
Brian, aged 15.

First it was garlic breath, then a sharp jabbing in my side. An umbrella had found its way into the tender area between my fourth and fifth rib, an area I reserve in my kindness for the pleasure of rush-hour sadists. Next came the inevitable tromp on my right foot. I looked down to see a large rubber galosh, its laces missing, its red border and empty eyelets leering back at me in smug victory. A fat leg connected the boot to a buffalo coat beaded with melted snow and smelling like a buffalo must smell when it forgets to wash. My eye was travelling up past the umbrella to the face when I remembered the garlic. Quickly I turned my head to the familiar and friendly ads. Red for the heart foundation, blue for Jay's corn salve, Only You Can Prevent Forest Fires! And just as I was about to lose myself in the happy juxtaposition of Panti-hose and Wonderbra, a lurching left turn reminded me of the umbrella, of 5 p.m. and the TTC* at its sardine best.

(*TTC: Toronto Transit Commission, operators of the transportation company.)

Brian had been diagnosed at age 14, as a severe schizophrenic. His psychiatrist recommended that he be kept in a regular school, rather than be institutionalized for treatment. "The Bus" is typical of his writing: imaginative, coherent, perceptive, entertaining, and always in accord with the "rules" of usage. Regrettably, his behavior could not be described as favorably. Be that as it may, Brian could write; better probably, than most of his teachers. It was his unpredictable behavior, and subsequently abysmal achievement record that put him in the slower learner class.

In the same class as Brian, was Sandra, aged 17.

Why People Enjoy Pets

There are lioal and loveade and hugable. There are like children. There sapasoateties cas talk and jump up and purr and big in nails.*

(*They are loyal and lovable and hugable. They are like children. They supposedly can talk and jump up and dig in their nails.)

Also in the class with Brian and Sandra and Bill, aged 14.

My Opinion of the Movie
(16mm version of "The Lady or The Tiger")

I think she gave that manager the money to tell her which door the lion was in to kill it. Then when her true love opened the door the lion would be dead and then he wouldn't be killed or he wouldn't have to marry the maiden. Or she could of killed the the maiden and then when she told him which door he would open the door and there would be only a dead maiden.

And in the same class, Glenn, aged 15.

Should Exams Be Abolished?

No, not in my opinion, if you can't take the "pressure" of an exam, what are you goind to do when you get out of school. Mortgage payments, rent payments, room & board.

How does one develop a writing program for classes of slower learners where the ability level covers such a broad range as this? (Perhaps the question should be asked: *Why* have a writing program at all? A response to this will come later in the chapter.) And what kind of writing program should a teacher attempt to establish? Consider how effective a lesson on a topic like *coherence* would be. Brian obviously doesn't need it. It would be utterly wasted on Sandra — and probably demoralize her. Bill and Glenn might benefit from such a lesson, but their needs seem more basic than this.

Perhaps drills in basic sentence structure might help. But a class of adolescents like this has already had years of this kind of thing. And it apparently does not make competent writers out of them. Or consider the time-honored programs which present writing, broken down into narrative, descriptive and expository divisions. Teaching these students such distinctions is a futile effort at their stage of development. Even if they understood the distinctions, what good — excluding the case of Brian — would it do?

A writing program for a slower learning class must therefore, take into account the reality that there is likely to be a great range of ability. Unlike regular classes this class usually does not have a common denominator of writing ability from which to build. There is little point in attempting to teach a specific lesson to the *whole* class.

Writing Program: Need #2

The opportunity to express one's "interior", without compunction and without fear of ridicule or retribution, must be part of any adolescent slower learner writing program.

My Pain
Liz, aged 15.

I slept in the same bed as you
Felt your warm breath against mine
Your long hair that touched my face
And your soft lips that were pressed against mine
Your body that covered mine like a warm blanket
The hands that touched me — that made
me feel different, secure
And made me feel like a woman.
But the lies
        And the hate
And a pill that told it all
And ended the beginning of a new life
And what's left is the bruises
And the truth that will be
held forever in my heart,
The pain, the hurt, the love
And a secret that will never
be forgotten.*

Imagine yourself evaluating Liz's piece of writing. What does one do? Give it an A? B+? D? 70? 23? Is a mark what Liz needs, or what she is looking for? And more difficult, what comment does one write on her paper? What does one *say* to her: "Needs punctuation"? "Good use of suggestion"? "A sensitive subject but rather unsubtle?" Liz, when she wrote this was making a confession; she was expressing a confidence.

---

* For three months, Liz carried on an affair with a 23-year-old married man. Both were on drugs. Liz became pregnant. The man ended the affair, and Liz had an abortion.

It was an emotional commitment, one that cannot be met with: "Good Work! Watch your commas! B+".

The writing of so many slower learning adolescents — and the distinction, *adolescent* is important here — is exactly like Liz's in purpose, if not in content. Here for example, is Maria, aged 15.

The Sixth Sense

> I feel when I'm with people that if there thinging somthing bad about me I know it. I know by looking at people if they hate me or not most people don't like me I want to be a singer but somthing tells me not to. I believe in God so maybe He tells me not to. If I don't read the Bible I'll have a bad drem it happen to me once. Somthing in me would like to change the world in the name of God but I cann't do it by myself. Something tells me not to be mean to people. Because I do like people, talking to them about God or anything. I believe that E.S.P. is God telling us whit to do, I know its true.

Like Liz, Maria is making a statement about herself, about the state of her soul. Her expression here is gentle, sensitive, and marked by that sad adolescent mixture of perception and confusion. No such confusion applies to Don, aged 14. He is slightly palsied, and has limited use of his left leg.

> It is time for you and I
> To become men
> And walk and love.
> Really
> It is time.

Don and Maria and Liz provide examples of a profound need in a slower learner's writing program: the therapeutic need to express one's *self*. The teacher of adolescent slower learners who has never seen this kind of writing, simply does not exist. Given the dominant social factors in a slower learner's background, it seems only natural that deep but unexpressed thoughts and feelings would build up. Yet textbook-oriented and drill-oriented programs provide almost no opportunity at all for a student to express what he really feels.

Usually a slower learning adolescent is either unwilling or unable to express his personal feelings verbally. But on paper, "unconfronted", and in the privacy of his own mind, a slower learner can make concrete those abstract feelings that build pressure in him. At his own pace he can use his writing to give shape and perspective to his emotions and inner thoughts. And at the same time he can literally "get them out" so they can be viewed more objectively, and perhaps, dealt with.

Writing Program: Need #3
The student must want to write, or at least, be interested enough to make a sincere attempt.

Sunset
Sally, aged 13.

As the sun sank slowly beneath the horizon, leaving its rich reds, golds, and oranges imprinted on the evening sky, the deep, dank mist began to creep around the meadow, already gripped in the folds of darkness.

Wind
Frankie, aged 14.

Sometimes a wind can turn me on. Wind is rose-fresh and face-rubbing, it lifts my hair and brushes it and takes my sleeve and tickles my arm. But the best part is what it dos inside. When I close my eyes it gos inside and builds there. Makes me forget everything. Like I said its just like turning on, only wind is clean.

Without missing a cliché, Sally has managed to present a passage that is consistently and flawlessly *dull*. Sally was an outstanding academic student, always leading the advanced class at examination time. She was gentle and kind, and her behavior was a model of that which most school systems hold dear.*

On the other hand, Frankie at age 14 was the leader of a slower learner class that was so disruptive it was regarded with awe by other students in the school. Sally's class was taught parts of speech, and writing techniques (such as use of adjectives). Frankie's class was given the program described later in this chapter. Both classes were tenth grade.

The fact that the piece by Frankie is obviously more interesting, more vital, than that written by Sally does not suggest that slower learners are more capable writers. It does suggest however, than an important factor in the results of any writing program is whether or not the students are interested in what they are writing.

---

* At the time of this writing Sally teaches English in a Canadian secondary school.

Sally was clearly going through motions. She was capable of much better work than what appears in "Sunset", but Sally like so many academically successful students had discovered how to play the game of "school", namely: *adherence to laid-on prescriptions is more important than originality or creativity.* That syndrome by the time a student reaches university is honed to a science, and the art of saying nothing is elevated to new heights. Note these examples from *one class* of my university students.

> I feel that "Snow" is a poem which has oversucceeded in its liberality of interpretations.

> Capitalizing on the potentialities inherent in poetic imagery and song forms, Joni Mitchell creates, in "Song To A Seagull", an underlying sense of tension and ambivalence.*

> The repetition of
>> My dreams with the seagulls fly
>> Out of reach out of cry,
>
> becomes almost a refrain which varies the theme by a slight twist of meaning with each reiteration so that the effect is incremental as the refrain accumulates a greater depth of meaning.

The famous teacher-literary critic Northrop Frye has pointed out that teaching a child to write by proceeding from word to phrase, from phrase to sentence, and from sentence to paragraph, is merely ensuring that what he eventually writes will be a dead language (Frye, 1972). Clearly, the previous examples bear this out. But what should be added to this observation of Frye's is that such prescriptive methods make the language even duller because they eliminate the *desire* to write.

With slower learners, this factor is even more important than with academically-oriented students. Given the slower learner's frequent inattention to detail, and his propensity for quitting when faced with a heavy task, his writing — if attempted at all — is even worse if he has to be *made* to write.

A slower learner going through motions in the same way that Sally did, would inevitably leave disastrous results. Frankie's paragraph, "Wind," is an example of what he could do when his best efforts were called for. In the particular lesson, Frankie and his classmates were responding to a series of 35mm slides depicting various beautiful effects of wind. And the poetic sensitivity of Frankie's paragraph is not unique.

---

* In a class of 29 students, 16 used the phrase "tension and ambivalence" in this assignment.

Almost the entire class responded in the same way. Yet that same class if given a formal lesson in, say, the technique of contrast would always respond poorly to the list of topics that inevitably follows such a lesson.

Writing Program: Need #4
The student must be given something to write about.

The following sentences were written by Vanda, aged 13. The instructions were simply to take a list of words and use each of them in sentences, attempting if possible, to connect the sentences into a paragraph. Vanda chose to ignore the second stage.

The paragraph that follows, "Being A Lady" is also Vanda's. Both the sentences and the paragraph were written within the same week.

1. The lady wear a casual dreess.
2. Charcoal is your in the barbecue.
3. The manoger has a big responsability in the store.
4. We use stov the cook to food.
5. The gils supper is extermely.
6. The hen and the roster got togather and had a fertil egg.

Being A Lady*

Being a lady is very important when you are around anybody. When people are talking you don't but in. When you sit down don't slam yourself down, sit down as if you are a ballet dancer. Don't sit at the table or any other place biting your nails. Also when you receive something you should always use your manners (no matter where you are you should always use your manners.) Be polite where ever you are too be.

In comparing Vanda's two efforts for level of usage and for quality of thought, there is little doubt which is better. And the reason is not hard to find. In the first piece, the sentences are an example of what happens when students are given words first, and then asked to find ideas for which the words can be used. In the second piece, Vanda is given the idea, and she must find the words to express it, the words to give it shape, dimension and clarity.

So many slower learning classes are taught writing by a programmed, or drill method. "Back to the basics" is usually the reason given. But the

---

* Vanda was a member of an all-girls class in which physical battling, rude noises and vulgarity were the mode. This topic was part of an informal behavior modification program that was reasonably successful.

fact is, such a method does not get back to basics at all, for surely ideas must be more basic than words. It is words (*pace,* psycholinguists) that give ideas shape. Since a slower learner's problem so often is a simple inability to communicate his ideas, it seems logical that to treat that problem, educators must work *from* his ideas.

There is yet another argument — usually advanced by educational elitists — that slower learners have no ideas. It is tempting to dismiss such a premise entirely, born as it is, out of ignorance. But there is a factor to be recognized. Because of their exceptionally negative self-image slower learners often feel that they in fact have no ideas, or that their ideas are not worth expressing. Years of experience in which the quality of their ideas has been compared unfavorably to those of brighter students have contributed significantly to this feeling.

An important feature of a writing program for slower learners then, is simply one that provides a subject from which ideas can be encouraged to grow, and be expressed.

And There Are Other Needs

If a writing program is going to be of any value to a slower learner, he must write often. Quantity is a vital feature. This is true in part because of therapeutic needs, and it is true because actual improvement in writing ability can only be realized *by writing.* Yet few teachers, even the most conscientious, have the time for the amount of evaluation and consultation necessary to make an impact.

A writing program must be functional. This is an axiom to which our society subscribes almost willy-nilly. Yet how functional must it be? How much formal writing have you, the reader had to do in the last month? (i.e. other than filling in reports or forms) Examine your local paper for employment opportunities likely to be filled by slower learners who graduate or who leave school early. How many advertisements call for *letters* of application? Ask any industrialist whether his workers write reports or whether they report by filling in forms. And just what is functional writing? Are an auto mechanic's functional writing needs similar to a television technician's, or a taxi driver's?

And finally, a writing program for slower learning adolescents must somehow accommodate the opportunity for a teacher to *talk* to students personally, and individually. This is necessary because few slower learners possess that objective, descriptive writing terminology that enables textbooks to talk to teachers (and a few academically successful students). Consequently teachers must suggest improvements literally "by ear". And personal consultation is necessary for slower learners simply to combat the "quit" syndrome. A word of praise or encouragement from an understanding teacher usually accomplishes more than pages of textbook drills.

How The Program Works

In operation, the writing program described below builds from the needs of individual slower learners. The students write frequently; yet teachers need not take home bundles of work to be evaluated every night. There is no predetermined sequence of drills; the teaching of a point in language or in writing can be done *when need* warrants it. And finally the program builds on a success formula. Teachers have opportunity to praise, personally, and students are able to see and sense their own progress.

Materials

Each student needs a writing workbook (wirebound or stapled) which he uses exclusively for this program. I have discovered the truth of the phenomenon Daniel Fader points out in *Hooked On Books**, that as a student's workbook fills, it acts positively on his sense of accomplishment with the result that the writing, both in usage and originality, improves significantly. The bound book also facilitates immediate comparison. By merely turning a few pages, a teacher can point out to the student his own progress.

The teacher should have a record book or diary with a full page devoted to each student. This record can be a teaching tool if no attempt is made to conceal it from the students.

The teacher will also find useful a set of interesting 35mm slides (optional) or posters (optional). Access to short 16mm film is useful (but again, optional). Mandatory, however, is a classroom set of books containing short prose articles, deliberately selected to interest the slower learning adolescent (not short stories, although occasionally these will suffice). From these materials come the stimulus, the desire to write, and the subject, the "something-to-write-about".

Prose articles are preferred over slides and films for a number of reasons. The latter media sometimes tend to be fleeting, or even confusing. Films sometimes create a mood of physical indifference. Slides, after the initial impact, tend to lose the quality of interest. Yet slides and films if used judiciously (i.e. sparingly) can be effective. Prose articles on the other hand, as well as short poems, do not suffer these

---

* Daniel Fader, *Hooked on Books: Program and Proof* (Berkeley Medallion Books, 1968.)

drawbacks. They are also effective in developing reading ability concurrently with the writing program. If a student has a piece of prose in front of him as a stimulus, he can always refer back to it for specifics. Short articles also allow the teacher to structure the specific assignment to a greater or lesser degree. For those students who have difficulty collecting their thoughts, a teacher can provide a few guiding questions, which draw the students' attention to specifics in the article.

Simple transcription sometimes helps students with a physical or a psychological handicap.* This is only possible with the article style of stimulus. Finally, if the prose articles are presented in a collection, there are inevitably extra pieces included for comparison, argument, amplification, extra reading, etc.

In Operation

1. Students must write regularly. Once a week or even more if possible. The frequency, of course, depends upon the teacher's judgment. (Note that this style of program is *not* a re-make of Fader's journal system.)

2. All writing is done in the bound workbooks. Whether the students take these books home or whether they are kept in the classroom depends again on the teacher's judgment. In my experience many slower learning adolescents come from homes where these books are frequently mislaid or abused. Such excuses as "My baby brother ate it!" or "The dog peed on it" are not uncommon. However, as the books fill with each student's own work, the incidence of loss decreases dramatically.

3. The first few minutes of the writing period are spent creating the stimulus and providing the subject. Here, the slides or film, or prose come into play.

Example

The following two selections are quoted from my book, *Prose of Relevance, Volume 1* (Agincourt, Ontario: Methuen Publications, 1971.)

---

* Sandra (see p. 34) at first joined all her letters together in one continuous line. The piece on p. 34 is her development after 3 months of transcribing to emphasize the need for word clusters.)

This text is designed for use by adolescent slower learners. The selections below are on the subject of extra-sensory perception.

> It was as though something actually pulled me away. I was eating lunch in the cafeteria with some of my friends when suddenly I *knew* my mother was in trouble in the kitchen somewhere. And that's why I just got up and ran to my locker, got my coat and ran home. I was so scared I don't even remember running, and I know I didn't get permission to leave the school. Of course, when I got home I felt like an idiot, because my mother was standing in the doorway looking at me as though I was nuts!
> It was at supper when she had the heart attack — just fell right over at the sink.
> p. 3.

> Jules Verne wrote *From The Earth to the Moon and Round the Moon* about 100 years before the famous Apollo 10 mission. The launch site that Verne chose for his fiction was Stone's Hill, Florida (about 50 miles from Cape Kennedy). His rocket ship took 97 hours, 20 minutes to reach the moon (Apollo 10 was 98 hours, 10 minutes). Verne's story had *three* astronauts; they all experienced weightlessness; splashdown was in the Pacific where they floated until picked up by special rescue boats.
> p. 17.

The teacher presents these articles, in whatever manner deemed most effective, and invites discussion by means of some questions prepared in advance. (Flexibility, of course, is essential.) At a critical point in the discussion, *not* after the topic is exhausted, the students are invited to react in writing. The degree of instruction at this stage, is up to the teacher. Some teachers often get interesting results simply by saying something like; "Write what you feel about this", or "Has this ever happened to you or someone you know?" Other teachers find it useful to be more specific, e.g. "Give three reasons why you feel the case of Jules Verne and Apollo 10 is just coincidence."

In fact, some teachers find it useful to provide a variety of instructions, adaptable to a variety of students. Flexibility is important. If a student should choose to write about Jules Verne, or rockets or his mother, or the feeding habits of snails instead of writing on ESP, it makes no difference. The point is only, that he *write!*

4. By this point, up to ten minutes — more or less — have passed. Once all the students are writing, and once the inevitable one or two who never seem to be able to get started are given some help and encouragement, the teacher then moves to *each student individually,* and discusses briefly the writing from the *previous writing period.*

For example, if today, students are writing about ESP, in the previous writing period, they may have been writing about their reaction to the film version of *Lord of the Flies*. The discussion therefore will pertain to this latter piece.

5. During this brief, personal discussion with each student, the teacher should attempt to accomplish *two* and *only two* things. The first is a word of praise or encouragement. The praise may be about the student's quality of thought, or originality of opinion, or about the steady improvement in usage — anything, provided the praise is sincere, and directed to the writing.

    The second point covered in this brief encounter is *one* suggestion to the student on how to improve his writing. It is important that a teacher resist the overwhelming urge to correct the mass of errors in spelling, punctuation, and usage that so often appears in a slower learner's writing. Give only ONE suggestion.

The selection that follows below was written by Jack, aged 14.

Lord of the Flies

Being stranded on this island is the most terrible thing that has ever happened to me. Out of all the boys on this island not one of us is capable of taking us into their own hands and try to lead us to some sort of safety and comfort.

We have all heard and talked about the beasty but only one person has acctually seen the beastie. Raulph, I think, is doing the right thing by going about his business. The beastie has not done any damage yet so I don't think they should wory about it.

Jack was letting his personal feeling interfere with his so called leadership. Instead of going out regularly and trying to hunt, he just stayed around the beach bragging about how he was going to get the pig, this time for sure.

Another thing he did wrong was to take the twins off the mountain to help him hunt. The fire they were loading after went out and made their rescuer from the island a failure. I think Raulph has every right to be mad at Jack.

A rapid skimming of Jack's work opens a number of areas for praise and encouragement. He made a mature analysis of the situation; his paragraph structure is reasonably sound; the variety in sentence structure is praiseworthy. But when a teacher has come to know a student, the thrust and nature of the praise is often affected by that teacher's perception of the student's particular needs. Any one of the above accomplishments are worthy of praise, but because Jack happened to be a strikingly unimaginative student, I chose to praise him, in this case, for the idea of writing in the first person. For Jack, such an original idea as including himself in the story was significant.

Then, in the area of suggestion-for-improvement, there are several areas from which to select. A teacher might choose spelling (Raulph, acctually, wory, rescuer). One might pick inconsistency (beastie, beasty). Or agreement (one of us . . . their own hands). But given the fact that Jack has been praised for his choice of first person narrative, he would probably be more "tuned in" to a suggestion-for-improvement in this area. Any teacher reading this piece would immediately pick up Jack's shift out of first person narrative, into third person, at the end of the second paragraph. This, then becomes the suggestion. A teacher then can merely point this out to Jack — gently. It will be very easy for him to see what he has done, and he will be able to make the necessary alterations not only at the end of the second paragraph, but also at those few other points where he has made the shift. (e.g. "Jack *was* letting his personal feelings . . . .)

It is worth noting too, that to *describe* this brief situation takes more time than the situation itself. Usually a teacher can make a sincere compliment, and go on to explain a recommended improvement, in about one minute.

6. In the record book, the teacher then notes quickly on the page devoted to Jack, the substance of today's discussion, namely, Jack's imaginative use of the first person, and the fact that he slipped out of this a number of times. The point of this is that during the *next* writing period when students are writing on yet another subject, the teacher will know as he comes to Jack, that what they are working on together is consistency in narrative point of view. (Although neither Jack nor the teacher would likely use that term.)

   With the student next to Jack, the teacher may choose to work on spelling, or sentence errors of some kind, or even a more delicate thing such as the student's propensity toward vulgarity if it applies. The vital feature is that the teacher deals with each student individually. Together, the teacher and student work on one writing problem at a time until over a few, or several, or many writing periods, that problem is overcome. Then another problem is selected. In this way, the student *sees* and experiences a sense of progress. Rather than having his piece of writing returned weeks after he wrote it, and dripping with the blood of his teacher's red marking pencil, the student is motivated by a positive sense of development.

A Summary

In frequent, regular, writing periods, the class is presented with a topic that, hopefully, is appealing. While they respond in writing to that topic, the teacher briefly visits each student individually. During a brief discussion the student hears an encouraging statement, and a suggestion for improvement. The teacher records both — particularly the suggestion — for ready reference in the next writing period, since teacher and student will now work together, on a single writing problem until it has been overcome.

Any Questions?*

"How can I 'get around' to *every* student, in one class period?"

Sometimes you cannot. However there are a number of factors which help. Usually classes of adolescent slower learners are smaller than regular classes (because administrators remember their own bitter experiences in slower learner classrooms). The usually high absentee rate in these classes often reduces the size even further. But occasionally to save time, a teacher can pass over individuals or groups of students with a comment like: "Your work was quite good last time, so I won't disturb you today." (But be sure to visit those students next time.)

"Do the students take their work home if they don't finish in class?"

Not unless the teacher suggests it. But usually such a requirement defeats the purpose of the program. The program is based on the *students'* needs, not the teacher's need for a series of completed assignments. Any student who wishes to take work home however, should be allowed to do so.

"Are students to rewrite their work?"

Only if they wish to. When the program is well along, and the students' workbooks begin to fill, the degree of voluntary rewriting increases significantly.

"What does one do with the student who finishes before the period ends? Or what does one do with the inevitable one or two who 'just can't write today'?"

The advantage of having a book full of interesting articles on broad themes is that students who finish early can be encouraged to read further

---

* This writing program has been implemented successfully in many areas throughout Canada. Since teachers often write or speak to me about incidental problems in operating the program, I have outlined the most frequent questions here. (KJW)

on the subject. Usually those students who "can't write today" merely need a start. If the teacher helps them get a first sentence written, this is often enough. Then too, there is the option of reading further on the subject, or even possibly, simple transcription.

Finishing early, or not-wanting-to-write, are logistical problems faced by all teachers of adolescent slower learners, no matter what program is used. But in a program such as this one, the incidence of such problems is measurably less.

"Do teachers take the work home to grade it?"

One of the basic features of this writing program is fulfillment of the need to write as often as possible. No teacher can possibly evaluate at home all the work the students do if they write as often as they should. The brief personal discussion with each writer *in class,* also helps to eliminate "red-pencil disease"; there is time to deal with only one error. Students learn to write by writing, not by constant grading.

"What happens when students are absent?"

Unlike the assignment style of writing program, a student can miss a writing period or even several. On the day he reappears, he will always have a piece of work to discuss with the teacher, from the last day he attended.

"How can one discuss improvement in writing when the students do not know any of the terminology?"

This question frequently tends to be more emotional than rational. Terminology, as a famous American novelist has put it, is the bastion of those who can neither write themselves, nor recognize the ability in others. Yet, the question cannot go unanswered, and there are two responses.

One: Adolescent slower learners have already — for several years — demonstrated their incapacity or profound unwillingness (or both) when it comes to learning traditional grammar with all its language. To remediate that problem is first of all a waste of everyone's time, and secondly, to treat the problem in any adequate way means there will be no time left for writing, or reading, or anything else of greater importance.

Two: How many adolescent slower learners make writing errors that can be described in the neat packaged terminology of textbooks? Rarely does a slower learner merely misplace a modifier. Usually he combines it with a fault in parallel structure, an error in punctuation, one in sentence structure and then spices the whole thing with an ellipsis that defies even supernatural perception.

How for example, would one use terminology to describe the errors in the following piece, assuming that the terms would even be understood by the kind of student who would write this way in the first place?

Our Exam System
Zachary, aged 14.

> I think we should keep the system we have this year. I like the idea about first term to have no exam and second term to have exams on work in third term you can keep your marks given to you or you can write. I think this is a happy medium you write exam and you have no exams so if you are no good in exams you have the term marks from the first term and third to pass you.

During the brief discussion, rather than use terminology, simply use the student's "ear". He knows what he wants to say. If he reads it aloud, or if the teacher reads it aloud, confusion in syntax will be revealed, and working together, it can be corrected. If the particular piece of writing is beyond "ear" comprehension, it is certainly beyond analysis by terminology.

> "Doesn't the stimulation time at the beginning of the period sometimes become so involved that it is impossible to have any writing done?"

Occasionally. This again is up to the teacher. There are many times when a wide-ranging discussion, giving opportunity for development of verbal fluency, listening, and generation of ideas, is more important than writing.

> "Are the students ever taught lessons in writing technique, or lessons in usage?"

Many teachers would accept the premise that there is little point in teaching writing techniques when students are not ready for them; or that teaching conventions (like punctuation) is redundant when students already handle them well. And most teachers would agree that adolescent slower learners rarely make *single, definable,* errors in a sentence. Hence, two real benefits grow from this writing program. First, students can be taught writing techniques when they are ready for them. The teacher knows they are ready because the program provides for widespread, intimate and *frequent* contact with the students' work. A second benefit is that the teacher can draw lessons on points of usage and conventions from the students' own work. A lesson, complete with drill exercise, can be presented using the student's own achievements — and errors — for material, avoiding artificial textbook drills that are concocted in isolation. This style of writing program is flexible enough for a teacher to built *into,* as well as build *from,* at the appropriate point in time.

"Should the students receive marks, or grades, or some kind of scaled evaluation?"

If both teacher and students agree that marks or grades are necessary, then of course there is no problem. Since most classrooms never achieve this state of nirvana, such simple solutions are rare. If for whatever reason, grades are to be assigned to these pieces of writing, then it seems only reasonable that these grades should work *for*, and not against teacher and student.

Adolescent slower learners are accustomed to poor or failing grades. And a high mark or grade rather than inspiring them, often makes them distrustful. To this paradox is added the teacher's own problem of rewarding original or logical thought that is expressed in less-than-adequate prose.

Therefore a system of granting *two* grades has proven to be a reasonable alternative. One grade is awarded for thought, and general content — effort. In this case the student is judged against himself. And a second grade is awarded for the quality of writing. In this case the student is judged against a more objective, but hopefully flexible, standard. The two-grade system accommodates both the student's and the teacher's *attitudes* about grades, while still maintaining a form of objectivity. The student's effort — or lack of effort — is rated honestly, and so is the writing. Most important is the fact that the system is encouraging. Instead of receiving consistently low marks for poor writing, in spite of strong effort, the students see their *efforts* rewarded accordingly. Usually, greater effort means a higher quality of writing too, and the student can develop a sense of his own progress as his *writing* grade improves.

In this way, grades and marks rather than reinforcing the cycle of non-effort and subsequent failure, can alternatively, develop a cycle of positive attitude and success.

And once an adolescent slower learner learns to think that he *can,* the road is wide open.

CHAPTER SIX

Developing Oral Fluency

Brian Powell* has represented Canada several times in the Olympic Games. He is a marathon runner who stays in condition by running at least twenty-five miles a day. In 1960, Brian arrived in Athens, Greece, at 4 a.m., went immediately to his billet, had his landlady write the address of the billet on a piece of paper, and hailed a taxi. The driver took him to the Parthenon where, in the bushes, he changed into his running shorts, and began his daily twenty-five mile practice run. All this in the dark of early morn.

He quickly became lost in the winding streets of Athens. His money, the address of the billet, and his identification were miles away in his clothes which he could not find. He could not speak Greek. Not only was Brian lost, but he didn't even know where he had come *from*! It was more than just a case of finding someone who would understand his predicament. He wasn't even sure what to explain!

I wish that every teacher of slower learners could have shared this experience!

Few teachers can fully appreciate the intensity of the adolescent slower learner's frustration at being unable to articulate orally — the deep agony of being unable to express feelings and opinions. Teachers, because they are usually orally fluent themselves, tend to forget how one's confidence, one's whole attitude to life is affected by the ability to articulate well. For many slower learners, school — and life — is, in fact, like living in a foreign country where the language is entirely strange. The frustration that a mathematics teacher feels when he cannot get his students to understand an "obvious" concept, the feelings of the English teacher who somehow cannot convey the "obvious" intent of a poet — these are the experiences of the adolescent slower learner on a day-to-day basis.

> There is no gift of speech; and the level at which people have learned to use it determines the level of their companionship and the level at which their life is lived. (J. H. Newsom, Report, *Half Our Future* (H.M.S.O., 1963), para. 330.)

> This matter of communication affects all aspects of social and intellectual growth. There is a gulf between those who have, and the many who have not, sufficient command of words to be able to listen and discuss rationally; to express ideas and feelings clearly;

---

* Author of *English Through Poetry Writing* (Heinemann, 1968) and *Making Poetry* (Collier-Macmillan, 1973).

and even to have any ideas at all. We simply do not know how many people are frustrated in their lives by inability ever to express themselves adequately; or how many never develop intellectually because they lack the words to think and reason. This is a matter as important to economic life as it is to personal living; industrial relations as well as marriages come to grief on failures in communication. (*Ibid.*, para. 43.)

Speaking is prerequisite to the child's development of a sense of identity. It is a *behavior** inseparably linked to the processes of thought and communication. Speech habits mirror the form and quality of one's thought, the nature of his social identifications, and the form and quality of his interaction with his physical environment and with other persons. Speech habits are important to vocational success and effective citizenship. Speech is thus *central* to the nature of man, to the development of the person, and to the functioning of political, economic and social institutions. ("The Field of Speech: Its Purposes and Scope in Education", Speech Association of America, 1963.)

The importance of one's speaking ability cannot be overestimated. It is an ability more natural to man than reading or writing. And as a factor in human endeavor, in human development, and in simple day-to-day functioning, the importance of speaking outweighs reading and writing by a considerable margin. Yet so many educators consciously avoid making oral programs part of a curriculum. No doubt this is an outgrowth of the fact that "talk" in education, is such a semantically charged word.

To many administrators, talk implies a discipline problem. On the theory that a good classroom is a quiet one, talk is suppressed rather than encouraged. Western culture of course supports this. Proverbs like "Silence is golden", "A closed mouth catches no flies", are part of our social fabric.

Teachers of English particularly, harbor a belief that writing is the communicative mode of a sophisticated, educated class whereas speech is the communication of the common man. Teachers — and even students occasionally — feel guilty when they spend a whole class period "just talking". In spite of the fact that many a teacher's best classes — those classes that end with the students still buzzing with interest as they leave the room — are those in which everyone has gone "off topic" and spent the time discussing, there is still a feeling of guilt, still a sense that next day "we must get down to work" to make up for "time *lost* in discussion".

(*italics mine. KJW.)

An intelligently directed and useful program in oral development, or discussion, or directed talk — whatever phrase is used — is of first importance to adolescent slower learners, especially in light of the home environment from which so many of them come. The information on students background as implied in the Toronto Survey (p. 17) is fairly representative. Given this kind of background, and taking into account the extremely useful work of Bernstein, Vygotsky and many others*, it is easy to see how closely interwoven are environment, language, and the slower learner's achievement in school.

Making An Oral Program Work

A classroom should be the safest place in the world to make a mistake. And creating this atmosphere is, above all else, the teacher's responsibility. This is the first requirement for a successful oral program: a safe atmosphere in which *all* students may contribute to a discussion, whether it is held in small groups, in pairs, or as a class.

A second necessary feature is that students must have something to talk about. Worthwhile, interesting and relevant topics will stimulate any slower learner to contribute. Preparing and structuring these subjects is the teacher's responsibility, either through the aid of a useful textbook which provides a variety of useful materials, or through his own resources. An adjunct to this requirement, of course, is a reasonable degree of variety, not only in subject material, but in the manner in which the discussion is structured.

Finally, students must learn about discussion itself. They must learn what is involved in good discussion, what cooperation and compromise mean, what the simple factor of listening entails — in short, the whole art of effective oral communication.

---

* B. Bernstein, "Some sociological determinants of perception", *British Journal of Sociology,* 9 (1958); "Language and social class", *British Journal of Sociology,* 11 (1960); "Social Structure, Language and Learning", *Education Research,* 3 (1961); "Social Class and Linguistic Development: A Theory of Social Learning", in *Economy, Education and Society,* eds. A. H. Halsey, J. Floud, and C. A. Anderson (New York: Free Press, 1961); "Aspects of language and learning in the genesis of the social process", *Journal of Child Psychology and Psychiatry,* 1 (1961).

L. S. Vygotsky, *Thought and Language* (Cambridge: M.I.T. Press, 1962).

Even more dramatic is the work of W. Goldfarb, "The effects of early institutional care on adolescent personality", *Journal of Experimental Education,* 12 (1943), and H. C. Dawes, "A study of the effect of an educational program upon language development", *Journal of Experimental Education,* 11 (1942), who found that institutional environments can have a profound effect on children's linguistic and intellectual development.

A Suggested Procedure

Step One: Here is an exercise that usually has dramatic results. It is effective in demonstrating to what extent most people assume rather than render their dialogue. And it demonstrates the wide gap between the speaker's intent and what the receiver interprets. The exercise makes a very effective beginning for an oral program.

> Use two sets of children's building blocks, of various shapes, colors and sizes. The sets must be identical in every respect. No more than 6 or 7 blocks are required.
>
> The teacher takes one set and builds it into a simple design. The other set remains untouched.
>
> A pair of students comes forward. One of the pair *must not be allowed to see the designed set.* He is given the undesigned set of blocks. The other student then describes the designed set, and his partner must attempt to duplicate exactly the design described. The student who is describing may do it one block at a time and must not look at what his partner is building. The student who is attempting to duplicate must not ask questions.

No amount of teacher-talk is as effective in making a point as this exercise. Rarely does the student who is building, come even remotely close to the design prepared in advance.

Step Two: (similar exercise) The whole class can be divided into pairs. Each student has a package of paper matches. One makes a design and attempts to describe it to his partner so that it can be duplicated.

This can be done without objects too — putting the hands together and interlacing the fingers in a design. The variety of exercises is unlimited.

Step Three: Cooperation to Achieve a Solution

1. Organize the students into small groups (5-6).

2. Give the groups this problem.

> What is the average height in feet and inches (or centimeters) of the members of this group? What is the average weight in pounds (or kilograms)? Any member not knowing his exact height or weight may estimate. There is a time limit.
>
> (N.B. Do not state what the limit is. The idea is merely to give a slight sense of urgency to the situation.)

3. Reconvene as a class for the answers to 2. After the answers are received, have each student in the class reflect upon privately, or write on a sheet of paper, responses to these questions.

    (a) Did the group have trouble starting? Why? or why not?

    (b) What were some of the things that slowed the group down?

    (c) Did anyone take over as leader? If so, did it help?

    (d) Did any member slow things down particularly? If so, *how?*

    (e) How might the group move more quickly next time?

4. (Most N.B.) Return to groups again. Each group discusses the questions in 3.

5. Follow up by holding a group discussion to calculate the average age in *years* and *months* of the members of the group. This time, invoke a *four* minute time limit, and announce this to the class.

Step Four: Teaching the Importance of Listening to One Another

1. Break class into small groups (5-6) and present them with a topic for discussion. Ideally, the topic should be at hand (i.e. a piece of writing); it should be on a controversial subject; and structured questions should follow it.

    An example of an effective piece, is this one from *The Population Bomb* by Paul R. Ehrlich.

Why Has The Population Problem Become A Crisis?

It has been estimated that the human population of 8000 B.C. was about five million people, taking perhaps one million years to get there from two and a half million. The population did not reach 500 million until almost 10,000 years later — about 1650 A.D. This means it doubled roughly once every thousand years or so. It reached a billion people around 1850, doubling in some 200 years. It took only 80 years or so for the next doubling, as the population reached two billion around 1930. We have not completed the next doubling to four billion yet, but we now have well over three and a half billion people. The doubling time at present seems to be about 35 years. Quite a reduction in doubling times: 1,000,000 years, 1,000 years, 200 years, 80 years, 35 years. Perhaps the meaning of a doubling time of around 35 years is best brought home by a theoretical exercise. Let's examine what might happen on the absurd assumption that the population continued to double every 35 years into the indefinite future.

    If growth continued at that rate for about 900 years, there would be some 60,000,000,000,000,000 people on the face of the earth. Sixty million billion people. This is about 100 persons for each square yard of the Earth's surface, land and sea.

Discuss

1. On the absurd assumption that 60 million billion people ever did live on the face of the earth, what are some of the methods of living they would have to adopt?

2. A teacher may choose to appoint an observer for each group. The observers do not participate, but sit with the group quietly noting the position each member takes in the argument. *NOTE:* The teacher must insist that everyone contribute at least *once* to the discussion.

3. After discussion has gone on for a brief while, have the groups break apart. Then *each* group member writes on his own paper, in short form, the position (or positions) taken by each of the other members of the group.

4. Briefly the groups reconvene. The observers state the various positions taken. Each member compares these with his own conclusions.

5. As a class, hold a teacher-directed discussion under such questions as:
   (a) Why didn't I listen?
   (b) Did the other person express his points clearly?
   (c) Was I more interested in arguing than in listening and learning?

It is very important that the students *discuss the art of discussion.* Needless to say, an oral program is designed to promote linguistic and intellectual development, to expand vocabulary and the ability to conceptualize and to stimulate interest. But it is also vital that students become aware of the many less obvious factors involved in oral communication.

Step Five: Achieving Consensus of Opinion
The following game is based on actual work performed at NASA in the U.S.A. It was devised by Professor Joy Hall, University of Texas School of Business Administration.

1. Distribute the following information to the class. Each student does it *on his own.*

You are in a space crew originally scheduled to rendezvous with a mother ship on the lighted surface of the moon. Mechanical difficulties, however, have forced your ship to crashland at a spot some 200 miles from the rendezvous point. The rough landing damaged much of the equipment aboard. Since survival depends on reaching the mother ship, the most critical items available must be chosen for the 200-mile trip. The fifteen items left intact after landing are listed below. Your task is to rank them in terms of their importance to your crew in its attempt to reach the rendezvous point. Place number 1 by the most important item, number 2 by the second most important, and so on through the least important number 15.

——— Box of matches

——— Food concentrates

——— 50 feet of nylon rope

——— Parachute silk

——— Portable heating unit

——— Two .45 caliber pistols

——— One case dehydrated milk

——— Two 100-pound tanks of oxygen

——— Stellar map of the moon's constellation

——— Life raft containing CO_2 bottles

——— Magnetic compass

——— 5 gallons of water

——— Signal flares

——— First-aid kit containing injection needles

——— Solar-powered FM receiver-transmitter

2. Break class into groups again, this time without observers.

3. The idea now is that each group must achieve a *group consensus* in ranking the importance of these items. *Each member of the group must be in agreement with each choice of ranking.* A simple majority vote is not permitted. Dissenting group members must be convinced or else they must convince the others. No group may proceed from #1 to #2 or from #2 to #3 until *all* group members agree. Each group member must enter the group ranking beside his own.

4. Establish a reasonable time limit.

5. After a reasonable length of time has passed, give them these answers.

15 Box of matches (little or no use on the moon)

4 Food concentrate (supply daily food required)

6 50 feet of nylon rope (useful in tying injured, help in climbing)

8 Parachute silk (shelter against sun's rays)

13 Portable heating unit (useful only if party landed on dark side)

11 Two .45 caliber pistols (self-propulsion devices could be made from them)

12 One case dehydrated milk (food, mixed with water for drinking)

1 Two 100-pound tanks of oxygen (fills respiration requirement)

3 Stellar map of the moon's constellation (one of principal means of finding directions)

9 Life raft (CO_2 bottles for self-propulsion across chasms, etc.)

14 Magnetic compass (probably no magnetized poles; thus, useless)

2 5 gallons of water (replenishes loss by sweating, etc.)

10 Signal flares (distress call within line of sight)

7 First-aid kit containing injection needles (oral pills or injection medicine valuable)

5 Solar-powered FM receiver-transmitter (distress signal transmitter, possible communication with mother ship)

6. Have each group discuss the following questions.

   (a) Did anyone feel forced to give in, even though he was positive he was right? Then why did he give in?

   (b) Would voting have been easier? More useful?

   (c) Did anyone take over as leader?

   (d) Did the group do better than individuals? Why or why not?

   (e) Did anyone stick to an opinion and turn out to be right? How did the group react to this person?

   (f) Did anyone in the group go along with everything? Is this good or bad?

For further techniques and ideas see *Learning Discussion Skills Through Games,* Stanford and Stanford, available through Scholastic Book Services, Richmond Hill, Ontario, Canada, or for further discussion material see *Prose of Relevance, Volumes 1 and 2.*

Step Six: By this time most slower learners are becoming aware of the more subtle factors in discussion, and at the same time are developing their own abilities in oral communication. However, it is usually a good idea to keep presenting topics which require not only thought and verbalization, but group cooperation and consensus. For example, the following selection presents a topic of considerable interest. Questions 1 to 5 give a structure for some wide ranging discussion. But question 6 reasserts the need for cooperation and compromise to achieve consensus.

Drivers, Cars and Accidents

To begin with, it is completely unrealistic even to talk about a foolproof and crashproof car. This is true because an automobile must still be something that people will want to buy and use . . . .

John F. Gordon,
President of General Motors,
October 17, 1961.

1. What assumption is Mr. Gordon making?

2. What are some of the safety features that have been incorporated into cars since 1961?

3. Is there anything unsafe about the car that you may own? Your family's car? Your friends'? If so, whose fault is it?

4. Why is it so necessary for cars to look good?

5. "You can tell a man that he's stupid, that his wife is ugly, and that his kids are dim-wits, and he'll probably laugh. But tell him that he's a poor driver and he'll fly off the handle." Why are men in particular so anxious to be known as good drivers? Are *you* a good driver? How do you know?

6. State the *six* most important characteristics of a good driver, *in order of importance.*

Step Seven: From this point on, most classes of slower learners are well into the groove of discussion. Most of the students have become aware of the respect and cooperation necessary for useful dialogue. Just as important perhaps, they have come to realize the importance of talk itself. Whereas many of them hitherto would have used talk as an avoidance technique in class, they now see its value.

The teacher's task now becomes one of providing a variety of topics and structures for oral classes. He becomes an advisor, coach, and judge — a facilitator of discussion more than a leader.

Some Suggestions For Variety

A. Conduct some sessions with the whole class acting together in a unit, perhaps with a student leader as chairman. For example:

The Knock-Out Blow

In May, 1965, Cassius Clay knocked out Sonny Liston for the heavyweight title. Clay himself said his knockout blow was a "twisting right-hand punch"; the referee (Jersey Joe Walcott) called it a "left to the jaw"; and sportswriters sitting at ringside reported it variously as a "tiny shot" or in one case, "no blow was landed".

Collect as many reasons as you can which might explain why such a wide variety of reporting can happen.

B. Have students work in groups and incorporate some writing into a specific, structured assignment. The example that follows can be expanded to include creative drama and various styles of interviews (sympathetic, confronting, etc.)

Situation

A group of policemen are lined up in front of a foreign consulate to protect it during a demonstration. As the demonstrators become more aggressive, they throw stones and garbage. The police respond by shouting warnings. In the crowd that has gathered to watch, a young mother foolishly allows her two-year-old to wander away from her into the danger zone. A policeman dashes out to pick up the little one and accidentally knocks over a demonstator who was going to do the same thing. This incident is the spark that turns the demonstration into a full-scale battle between police and demonstrators.

Assume the following roles:
1. One person writes the *police report* of the incident for his sergeant.
2. Another person in the group (a reporter) writes an eyewitness account of the incident for his newspaper. He is influenced by the fact that his father and two brothers are policemen.
3. This reporter hands over his copy to an editor who that morning was given a speeding ticket, and the day before had been told by his superiors that the paper was not selling well enough — that it did not have enough "interest". The editor makes some changes in the story.
4. One person interviews the demonstrator who was knocked over.
5. One person interviews the policeman who knocked over the demonstrator.

C. Debates, informal and formal, can be built out of such situations as the following:

Situation

You are suddenly witness to an act of vandalism. As you walk home from school, you see three boys smashing tombstones in a large public cemetery. One of them you clearly recognize as the only son of Mr. X who employs your father. Your father recently lost an arm in an accident, so Mr. X found him an easier job within the company. Mr. X also paid your father's salary while he spent six months in hospital. What do you do? If you told your father, what should *he* then do?

D. Utilize the "fishbowl" technique.

A group of four or five students discusses a particular topic such as the one that follows. The situation is different this time, however, because outside the circle of debators, there is another circle of silent observers.

Each observer is carefully watching *one* of those students talking. After a reasonable length of time has passed, the discussion is terminated, and each observer meets with his particular subject from the inner circle (or fishbowl) and explains to that person, observations he has made about that person's conduct, attitude, manner, etc., during the discussion. The following topic is effective for "fishbowling" because it so frequently stimulates the urge to digress with personal anecdotes, cruel humor, and other diversions.

My Brother Was Deaf

The poor little guy liked the other kids, although God only knows why; they tortured him. They called him "Dummy!" It was always "Hey Dummy!" this, or "Hey Dummy!" that, and he would just smile at them and walk over as if he didn't believe they were going to do something dirty to him. It was the only way he had of telling them he wanted to be their friend, but to them the smile just proved he was a "dummy".

One of their favorite tricks was to pretend to play hide-and-seek with him, and then when his back was turned they'd smash someone's window and run. The first he knew what happened was when some angry adult would be whacking him with a stick. Sometimes they'd play hide-and-seek with him and just take off. He'd hide someplace forever until I had to go find him and bring him home for supper.

Sundays were terrible. He loved to dress up and go to high mass. He couldn't hear anything of course, but he must have liked the smell of incense and the sight of all the ceremony. But he came home every time, covered with mud. They'd even pelt him *before* he got to church.

It's funny. Even the nicest kids on the street were mean to him. All he had to do was give them that silly little smile and it seemed they couldn't resist being cruel.

Gene T. (student) *Prose of Relevance 1*, p. 126.

Is it true that young people are more cruel than adults?

E. Panel Discussions. These can be planned or spontaneous. Either way, they are most successful when the moderator allows the class to ask questions or challenge statements.

Building the Groups in a Class of Adolescent Slower Learners

The *first* time a class of adolescent slower learners works in groups is very crucial. This time will set the tone for subsequent group discussions. Hence it is reasonable to follow a few successful practices for this one time at least. The suggestions below are useful.

For the *first* group discussion:

1. Teacher appoints the groups.

2. Assuming that there will be five groups, pick the five most extroverted students, or at least the five most likely to conduct a group with some confidence. Make each of these a chairman.

3. Pick the five most perceptive or most successful students and put one of these in each group.

4. Pick the five least perceptive and put one of these in each group.

5. Complete the group with the remaining students in the class, according to your best judgment of their *compatibility*.

6. Meet with the chairmen in advance, to explain their responsibilities and their rights.

7. Spend a considerable amount of time explaining to the class its responsibilities, and specifically, its responsibilities to the chairmen.

8. Discourage note-taking for this first session,

9. Be certain that students do sit in a circle. The dynamic of a group will not function unless each member can see *all* the others.

10. Do *not* insinuate yourself into a group, but be available to answer questions. At the end of the first session of discussion, make a five-

minute presentation in which you present some of your observations. Be certain that you make specific mention of a good idea presented in each group.

After students have worked in groups successfully, *once*, usually any structure will be successful.

CHAPTER SEVEN

Teaching the Adolescent Slower Learner to Listen

Try this listening experiment on a group of adults, and on a group of adolescent slower learners. The results will almost assuredly be the same for both groups. Ask the group to pay attention because you are about to give them a situation. Tell them that note-taking is optional; they may simply pay attention in whatever way they usually do. The situation:

> You're a bus driver and at the first stop two men and two women get on. At the second stop one man gets on and one woman gets off. At the third stop one man gets off and two women get on. One child gets on. At the fourth stop a man with a dog gets on. Two children get on. What is the name and address of the bus driver?

Most people are fooled by this little test for a number of reasons. Some concentrate on data and miss the main point. Others do not *begin* listening in time. Some dismiss the situation as foolish or irrelevant; other dismiss it because it contains arithmetic and they "aren't able to do arithmetic". All these reasons are linked to listening *behavior*. And if there is one area in which the adolescent slower learner shares an apparent weakness with the rest of the world, it is poor *listening behavior!*

Some False Assumptions About Listening

Many of the inaccurate beliefs about the subject of listening have been exposed for a surprisingly long time. The first of these beliefs is the incredible attitude that listening is unimportant. The oft-quoted Rankin survey, completed in 1939, used adults of various occupations and found that on average, 70% of their waking day was spent in verbal communication: 9% writing, 16% reading, 30% talking and *45% listening!* (At the same time, Rankin, who did his research in Detroit, Michigan, discovered that in the Detroit public schools, reading received 52% of the time in the classroom, while listening got 8%.)

A more dramatic survey (Bird, 1954) was based on a specialized occupation: dieticians. The results (using 110 dieticians in 48 states of the U.S.A.):

reading 4%
writing 11%
speaking 22%
listening 63%

Other false assumptions have been handily toppled by the work of Dr. Ralph Nichols at the University of Minnesota. Nichols' research shows that we have exaggerated the connection between intelligence and listening. His work also shows that the belief that learning to read will automatically teach us to listen is not completely valid.

Particularly interesting was an informal project carried out by Nichols and a large group of American teachers. Nichols had the teachers agree to stop at some point in a lesson; say "Time Out"; and then ask two questions:

1. What were you thinking about?
2. What was I talking about just before I called time out?

Nichols found that on average, 90% of the first grade pupils were listening, and 80% of the second grade. Students in the seventh and eighth grades dropped to 43.7% and by high school the average dropped to 28%!

Yet in the face of such depressing statistics, Nichols also found that listening *can* be taught, and that one of the first stages — and most important — in this process is making people *aware* of their aural deficiencies. This step is doubly important for adolescent slower learners.

Why Listening For Slower Learners?

Because they can become *good* listeners. Since intelligence (or at least "schooltype" intelligence) and listening are not absolutely interdependent, and since listening occupies such a major portion of our communicating activity, it seems sensible therefore that a listening program should become an integral part of a slower learner curriculum. Such a program would necessarily emphasize the behavioral aspect of listening. By the time of their adolescence slower learners with their negative self-image and strong tendency to avoid or reject anything that is not immediately appealing, have usually become notoriously bad listeners. That is, their listening *habits* are bad ones. A course in listening then would be designed to make them aware of these bad habits. Emphasis should be placed on what listening is all about, rather than on such things as "how to listen".

Introducing The Program To Students

Here are three exercises which usually provide dramatic demonstrations of how poorly people listen, and how easily a communication becomes confused. They can be quite useful as an introduction to some work on listening, for they provide a basis for discussing listening habits.

I

Divide the class into groups of six (approximately). Each group numbers itself from one to six. The teacher gives the piece of information below to the number one in each group. The information is on paper. Each number one studies it briefly, gives it back to the teacher, and then repeats it to the best of his ability, to number two. This is done in a whisper. Two tells three, and so on. Then each number six repeats it into a tape recorder, or writes it on paper and then reads aloud. After the class has heard each number six, the teacher presents the original.

> Mary Louise lives in Berlin in a rented house with her five children — three boys and two girls — and her husband Basil. Her husband is a tyrant and refuses to take the family anywhere except on Sunday afternoons when he takes them out and drives at 80 or 90 miles an hour. So far though, he's managed to get them home without an accident.

II

This is a variation of exercise I, but more interesting to observe.

Maintain the group arrangement of exercise I, but send each number six out of the room. Then read the following passage to the rest of the group. They may or may not take notes. Then bring one of the number six group back to the room; select a member of the class who heard you read the passage, and have him or her repeat the passage to this number six. Then call in a second number six, he hears the passage from the first number six, and so on. (The exercise is much more effective if it is tape recorded.) The point here is that students can *observe* the deterioration of a passage as it moves from person to person.

Food Raids by Brazil Peasants

BRASILIA (Reuters) — Thousands of starving peasants are invading towns in drought-stricken northeast Brazil and breaking into stores and homes in search of food.

Official sources say about 200,000 people are on the move in the northeast, victims of a drought which has driven them from their homes in search of work as well as food.

Six freight trains have been held up and robbed of food supplies during the last week in the area around the coastal city of Fortaleza, 1,400 miles northeast of Rio de Janeiro.

The incident described above, occurred early in 1970.

III

Exercise III may be less dramatic than the first two, but it provides an effective springboard from which to begin the program itself.

Without telling the students what you are planning, deliver a two minute or three minute *prepared* lecturette at the beginning of a period. The subject must be something in which you are sure they have no interest.*

At the end of the period give the students a brief multiple choice comprehension, or true-false test on the subject.

Repeat this procedure on the next day, but this time be certain that the subject is one of real interest.

Lead a discussion on why most students probably did better on the second test than the first. Expand this into a discussion of *why* people do or do not listen. For example, some of the bad habits include:

1. Automatic dismissal of a subject as too difficult.
2. Premature dismissal of a subject as uninteresting.
3. Yielding easily to distractions.
4. Reacting negatively to the speaker.
5. "I-get-the-facts-only" listening.
6. Faking attention or not paying attention.
7. Getting over-stimulated and wanting to challenge or expand the speaker's point.
8. Making an over-detailed outline.

At this stage, a teacher can bring in exercises and practices in the various styles of listening behavior demanded of adolescent slower learners. These practices can relate directly to the students' present situation, or to a possible future situation.

The various ideas that follow, need not necessarily be presented in sequence. The determining factor of course, is the teacher's perception of the students' needs.

Practice In Straightforward Comprehension

Present several selections of prose. These should be recorded on audio tape, and in a voice *other* than the teacher's. The selections at this stage should be strictly *informative-expository,* with no attempt to slant opinion one way or the other. At the same time however, they must be relevant and interesting in order to stimulate the desire to listen.

Each selection should be followed by a series of comprehension questions designed to test not only the students' ability to listen and

---

* My personal favorite is the care of tuberous begonias (KJW).

recall, but also their listening styles. A sample series of questions follows, based on the selection on "Poltergeist" in *Prose of Relevance* 1, p. 22 ff.

Poltergeist

A most peculiar phenomenon that periodically seems to occur in people's homes is that of the spontaneous moving of furniture or other objects, often together with strange sounds such as knocking, footsteps, or a piano playing, whether or not there is a piano in the house.

Called *poltergeist* from the German: *geist* — spirit, *polter* — that makes an uproar, many people discount reports of it as the ramblings of a weak mind. As far back as 1570 Ludvig Lavater wrote:

If a worm which fretteth wood, or that breedeth in trees, chance to gnaw a wall or wainscot, or other timber, they will judge they hear one softly knocking upon an anvil with a sledge.

To add further doubt to the reality of poltergeist, it is most often associated with, and reported by young people, usually girls. Also, a poltergeist's activities are usually more mischievous than harmful.

Typical of the manifestations of the poltergeist are the following:

(a) noises or knocking on walls and ceilings, and footsteps on floors and staircases — all without apparent origin;

(b) uncontrolled movement of objects (telekinesis) apparently in defiance of gravity. Moving furniture and the hurling of small stones are common;

(c) disappearance of small objects to be discovered later in strange places;

(d) occasionally, arson.

Despite the fact that poltergeist invites scoffing and disbelief, some prominent people have acknowledged its possibility. The Roman historian Livy recorded showers of stones in the sixth century B.C. Saint Cyrian in 530 A.D. described an incident in considerable detail. Robert Boyle, a physicist and discoverer of Boyle's Law, was witness to the experiences of a minister in France, and John Wesley, the founder of Methodism, frankly expressed belief in the poltergeist which plagued his family home.

Even in the twentieth century, prominent and educated people have described their awareness of seemingly impossible sounds and movement, and to this day, houses in both Canada and the United States stand empty, unoccupied because of apparent poltergeists.

The following account is a report of a poltergeist that is more troublesome than most but it is fairly typical in many respects.

Ghostly Furniture-Moving Force Hangs Over Boy, 11

St. Catharines — Researchers of the supernatural may be asked to investigate reports of a ghostly force that is apparently directed against an 11-year-old boy here.

Policemen, lawyers, doctors and priests are reported, on different occasions in the boy's Church St. apartment, to have witnessed:

A bed on which he was sleeping tip onto its edge after it rose off the floor;

A chair he was sitting in overturn after floating about 7 inches off the floor, trapping him against a wall;

Furniture moving across the room and doors opening although no one touched them.

The ghostly force only demonstrates its presence when the boy is home, and it appears to be directed only at him.

However, nobody is willing to talk about the phenomenon. The boy's parents, neighbors, the witnesses and police refuse to publicly divulge any details.

Rt. Rev. Thomas J. McCarthy, Roman Catholic Bishop of St. Catharines, said he had received a report of the phenomenon from two parish priests.

"I don't think there is any trickery," Bishop McCarthy said. "A lot of things happen that haven't been explained."

The family has lived in the second-floor apartment for nearly 10 years, but the eerie events started only three weeks ago.

A woman in the apartment yesterday said that the family had gone to Montreal.

Inspectors from various public utilities have failed to find any logical reason for the furniture moving around the apartment.

One inspector suggested that an expert in the field of the supernatural might be called in to investigate.

A constable said he didn't turn in a report of what he had seen or his conclusions. "Everybody would have thought I was crazy."

Similar cases of mischievous ghosts, called poltergeists, moving furniture have been reported far back in history.

One feature that nearly all have in common is the presence of a young boy or girl.

1. Which of the following is *not* a typical manifestation of poltergeist?
   (a) The appearance and movement of small stones.
   (b) Small puddles of water which appear and disappear.
   (c) Doors opening and closing with no one near them.

2. One of the following people has *not* acknowledged the possibility of poltergeist.
   (a) John Wesley

(b) Robert Boyle

(c) Joseph Lister

(d) Thomas McCarthy

3. Write True or False.
   According to the information given in the article, a poltergeist's activities are not harmless.

4. Write True or False.
   The strange events in the St. Catharines home have been in fact witnessed by several responsible adults of various professions.

5. One of the following statements about the family in St. Catharines is not based upon evidence in the report.
   (a) They are probably Roman Catholics.
   (b) They are newcomers to St. Catharines.
   (c) Only the eleven-year-old boy has experienced poltergeist.

Analyze as a class, some of the results of the comprehension questions, trying to decide why or why not the answers were right or wrong. (Many students miss the preceding question 4 because they are still struggling with the tricky difficulty of question 3 and forget to listen.) Discuss how students might listen better, by making mental summaries, by getting the *main* points. It is very important that students be given several exercises of this type before going on to practice in other styles of listening.

Practice In Listening To Instructions

Usually, when one is given instructions on the job, or in any situation, there are certain presumed factors, for instance, knowledge of the immediate environment, names of associates, etc.

On tape present the following:

> You are a stock boy in a large department store; the store manager gives these instruction to you.
> "Go to the stockroom and get a case of 2½ inch Rubberset paint brushes. Put as many as you can into the display on the second floor, and put the rest in the shelves underneath. Then go to the small appliance repair shop on the third floor and pick up all the irons that have been fixed; take them to the mail room in the

basement, and pack them. Be sure to pack them in styrofoam. Then go to the shipping dock; they'll need your help there."

In the subsequent discussion, have several students state explicitly what they would do. Then, if someone does not bring this up, introduce the idea that an employee such as a stock boy would already know certain things (where to put the brushes that would not fit into the display; the location of the mail room.) Accordingly, a listener here has to pick up *for sure,* certain vital details, such as the size and brand of paint brushes.

Practice In Listening For Vital Details

Many listening situations are such that if a listener grasps only *some* of the information, he will still understand. Other situations are such that a listener *must* get certain details whereas others are unnecessary.

Try this one on audio tape.

The truck is loaded and waiting for you, but the deliveries will take all day. Here are the invoices with the information. The Westinghouse range goes to 17 River Road; the fridge goes to 314 Albany Cres., and the combination freezer-fridge goes out to the country. It's a farm in Minto township. Go east on Hwy. 4 to concession 8; turn right, and it's the second farmhouse on the right after you cross a big steel bridge.

The important fact to realize is that of all the information given in these instructions, the only part that *demands* exact recall is the instructions in getting to the farmhouse. The rest is on the invoices.

At this point, have students compose situations such as those above, and try them on one another.

"I-Get-All-The-Facts" Listening

The object of this unit is to demonstrate the danger of listening exclusively for facts, at the expense of the over-all impression. The following two stages are usually effective.

1. Present the bus driver story. Be sure that it is read slowly and clearly, without emphasis.

2. In order to demonstrate how details and statistics can obscure the main point of a passage, present several short pieces that are filled

with statistical information. Follow these with comprehension questions that deal with inferences and principles *rather than* facts.
(Be sure to do steps 1 and 2 in the same time period so that students can make comparisons and analyze their own listening habits.)

Into-The-Rut Listening

Have the following lists, with instructions, put on tape (preferably by a voice other than your own).

1. In the following lists, one word does not belong: What is that word?
   lumber
   plywood
   nails
   panelling
   glue
   radiator*

2. kerchief
   shirt
   pants
   umbrella*
   socks

   Now follow with the third list. You will find that most listeners have behaviorally adjusted themselves to listening for an item which differs in *nature* and *purpose* from the others.

3. pansy
   tulip*
   peony
   poppy
   petunia

   After a brief discussion, allowing the listeners to discover why they didn't "get" list three quite as quickly, present list four.

4. What two words do not belong?
   frolicsome
   fulsome*
   burdensome
   loathsome*
   cumbersome
   In this case the number of syllables is the determiner.

71

Note that the main purpose of this exercise, as with all the others is to demonstrate further how one's listening behavior affects one's reception. Accordingly, at this point, it is a good idea to have the *students* make up lists similar to those above. Such activity not only provides further practice, but by *doing,* the students understand better, the point that is being made.

Filter-Listening For Propaganda Techniques

This is probably one of the most important styles of listening in this age of bombarding mass media. Some of the following propaganda techniques are typical, and worth examining not only for their effect on students, but also because of the students' own use of them.

1. *Name Calling* ("Commie", "Fascist", "racist", "stupid")

2. *Glittering Generality* ("freedom-loving", "hard-working")

3. *Transfer* (Giving the impression — whether it is true or not — that the speaker's cause is supported by various authorities such as church, government experts, etc.)

4. *Testimonial* (A speaker cites testimony from a well-known person; or a well-known person such as a movie star may give testimony for something about which he is entirely ignorant.)

5. *Plain Folks* (A speaker deliberately adopts the status and attitudes of a group to achieve his point.)

6. *Card Stacking* (Never revealing an opposite point of view — or admitting that one exists.)

7. *Band Wagon* ("Look how many other people are doing it!")

Other techniques in oral persuasion are: flattery; appeals to fear, hate, discontent; the creation of devils on whom to place blame; constant repetition; use of rumor and half-truths.

Generally, it seems more effective to have students discover these techniques in operation, rather than to present them in a list. However, it is often a good idea to present a few techniques to get them started.

A practice passage follows.

Why Don't The Poor Work?
by a man making over $20,000 a year

The owner of more newspapers than anyone else in the world was stone broke at one point in his career. One of Canada's wealthiest mineowners came to Canada as a near-penniless immigrant. A considerable percentage of all the wealthy men in North America today began with nothing but initiative and ambition. Why can't the poor do the same?

Most of the poor just sit and moan about their state. And then they have the nerve to complain if the welfare cheque is late. Why should the rest of the world have to support them when all they do is sit around?

Instead of giving the poor money, give them jobs. Welfare can be earned. Every city has parks that need care, streets that need maintaining, or snow to be shovelled. Why can't the poor be paid to do this instead of being given money for doing nothing?

Sociologists say we shouldn't apply middle-class standards to the poor — that just because we think it is noble and honorable to work, we need not force our way of doing things on them. Well that's fine. I agree. If the poor don't want to work, then let's not have any middle-class money, earned by middle-class work, spent on them. We'll play our game; they can play theirs. And if they don't like that, they can shut up and spend our money the way we want them to.

It is usually a good idea when dealing with propaganda techniques to let the students open their books and *read* the article after listening to it and discussing it. This enables them to *see* what they might have missed *audially*.

Listening Over Distractions

Another stage which some teachers like to develop is practice in listening over distractions. For example, a passage is read on audio tape over a steadily increasing volume of background noises — conversations, radio, television, domestic noises, traffic.

Students are then asked to verify a selection of statements as actually having been taken from the work they have just heard. Some of the statements will be quoted verbatim from the passage. Others will be distortions of what is stated in the article. Careful listeners will be able to make the distinction.

Some Thoughts

1. There are many other techniques available to a teacher. Students can make charts in which they analyze their listening habits. They can hold practices in paraphrasing. They can be given exercises in semantics. (Use the word *run* in ten different ways.) They can analyze physical movement as a factor in delivery and listening. There are many useful

activities in a listening program. The degree of emphasis as always, depends upon the teacher's view of the students' needs.

2. Each item or type of listening presented in this short course is only a sample. It is expected that teachers using a particular item will develop further samples of the same type if the class needs the practice.

3. Experience shows that this style of course is more effective if done in periodic units over an extended length of time. Covering all areas consecutively does not accomplish the behavioral impact one should seek to achieve in such a course.

USEFUL BOOKS

Bird, D. E., "Have You Tried Listening?" *Journal of the American Dietetic Association.* March, 1954.

Nichols, R. G., and Stevens L.A., *Are You Listening?* New York: McGraw-Hill, 1957.

Rankin, P. T., "Listening Ability". Proceedings of the Ohio State Educational Conference. Columbus: Ohio State University, 1939.

CHAPTER EIGHT

Reading and the Adolescent Slower Learner

Fantasy #437

Lights come up on what is obviously going to be a board of directors meeting. The room appears futuristic: unusually shaped plastic furniture; stark metal sculptures; indirect, cold, lighting. On the rear wall, a gold-lettered plaque identifies the organization:

W. E. (C.O.N.)
World Educators
(Committee On Nonreading)

Four people sit opposite each other in pairs. Their obvious nervousness, and their sense of anticipation grates on one another. Clockwise from downstage right they are:

R.C. (Reading Consultant) a striking woman in her late thirties. Normally she is in control of most situations. The fact that this is not the case now, increases her agitation.

R.M.S. (Reading Machine Salesman) a tall, thin man, teetering on the brink of middle age. His most obvious feature at this point is his unbelievably mobile face.

R.T.W. (Reading Test Writer) the calmest of the lot, and the youngest. She is a trifle plain, and her manner of dress emphasizes this fact.

C.T. (Classroom Teacher) a man whose age is difficult to determine. He is rather fat and flushed, and his facial expressions show his obvious distaste for what is about to transpire.

The audience has about ten seconds to grasp this situation, when R.C. gets up, goes over to the wall and tears a page off a huge calendar. It is December 7, 2041.

No sooner does she return to her seat when C. enters. (C. is Chairman of W. E. (C.O.N.). This is a dramatic high point and C. knows it. He is an obvious executive, one who is always in control. With two long strides he is in his seat. The others murmur deferential good mornings, how are you, etc.

C.   All right! We suspected there was a leak. Now we know!

He passes out copies of a front-page newspaper clipping.

R.M.S.   I'll tell you it sure couldn't have been one of our people; we've got too much —

R.T.W.   *(To R.M.S.)* Surely you couldn't think it was us! We —

C.   Forget that! We'll find the leak; WE (CON) is no ordinary organization. Our problem is right here. *(He slaps the newspaper clipping.)* Let's get to it!

R.C.   You've got a plan?

C.   Maybe. But first let's assess the damage.

R.C.   If you want to see damage go look at my desk. There's a telephone message lying there from every administrator in my school district.

R.M.S.   I'm afraid of the stock market report. The bottom will drop out of our shares!

C.T.   *(In a small voice, more to himself than to the others)* I wonder what the students will do when they read this!

R.T.W.   Really? *(Ingenuously)* I didn't know any of them ever read a newspaper.

R.M.S.   Don't be silly. Of course they do. It's our own fault actually. We've been spending all our time convincing kids they can't read *books.* We should have been working on newspapers too. And magazines, and joke books, sex books, signs, automobile manuals, and all those other things they read in spite of us.

C.T.   *(With a little more confidence)* What's so bad about that? As long as a kid is reading . . . .

R.M.S.   What's so bad! What's so bad! Are you kidding? There's a whole industry at stake here! When the news gets around that kids *actually can read,* dumb kids included, we're out in the street, buddy!

C.   Now calm down. *(to C.T.)* R.M.S. is right. We've got to do something to save the reading industry. Thanks to our leak, whoever it may be, the truth is out — and there it is right on the front page.

He reads aloud.

'ADOLESCENT STUDENTS *CAN* READ. An unidentified official of W.E. (C.O.N.) today opened hidden files to reporters of the Associated Press revealing research which showed that adolescent students can and do, in fact, read. The real surprise reporters found, was that this research included adolescent slower learners. For years reading in the schools has been an emotional issue but now it . . . .' *(He begins to stutter.)* Oh hell! I can't go on! It's just that — well dammit — here *(getting very loud now)* — the thing that really blows it all, is that we had the kids *convinced* they couldn't read! Years of building up their fear and apprehension about reading — all blown in one lousy news story.

R.T.W. *(Sensing the need to contribute)* I don't think the situation is so far beyond rescue. Why don't I simply design a brand new reading achievement test? You know — all the usual stuff: passages of no interest to adolescents; vague and difficult questions; work in the odd passage that may be offensive to black kids or to some large ethnic group; emphasize white middle-class culture; don't give them enough time; that kind of thing. At least we'll get the slow learners.

R.C. C'mon. You did that all through the twentieth century. Remember, you can fool some of the peop . . . .

R.M.S. Spare us! *(He ignores R.C. and speaks to the others.)* Maybe she's right though; maybe we've worked the test thing into the ground. Y'know machines are the answer. How do you think we sold all those reading machines in the last century in spite of what research told educators? Now I've got an idea for a new . . . .

R.C. *(Clearly stung by R.M.S.'s snide remark)* Your machines are a pain. How does following a little light help slower learners? After a week on your machines, the only way they'll try a book is with a flashlight!
Look. *(To everyone in general)* Your proposals are too tangible. *My* people would be a safer bet. As consultants, we have access to an unlimited source of abstract problems. We'd just have to dig up a few more of these; resurrect some reading jargon we haven't used in a while — you know — stuff like kinetic linear progression and all that, and it won't be long before we can have everybody convinced again that kids can't read.
And besides there's never enough of us anyway. All we ever have time to do is *identify* problems. Nobody has time to do anything about them.

C. *(After a studied pause)* You may have something there! *(His anger is slowly replaced by a controlled excitement.)* We haven't worked the inner city reading problem thing for a long time either. And then there's native Indians. That's a whole field we've never touched! Say! I've got a press conference this afternoon and . . . . *In his excitement he spills a cup of coffee. For a minute the conversation stops.*

C.T. *(Has hardly looked up at all, ventures very quietly)* Why don't we just let the kids read, now that they may think it's possible? *(There is dead silence. Shock dominates the room. C.T. blushes slightly and adds)* I know kids *like to read* — even slower learners. Maybe with the fear gone they might just . . . .
No one moves. C.T., embarrassed now, stops talking. Slowly C. gets up. He walks over to a small table, pauses for a second or two reflectively, shakes his head, and presses a button. Almost immediately, two burly men in white appear through a side door. They respond to C.'s simple gesture, and with the efficiency born of practice, gag and remove C.T. in what appears to be a single motion. As C. returns to the table, the others nod at him understandingly. R.C. gets up to pull down a wall chart, and the lights fade.

FINIS

Ridiculous, of course. But even amid the hyperbole of that scenario, there are a few realities that must be recognized by any teacher who hopes to encourage adolescent slower learners to read.

In the first place, there *is* a reading industry. A brief glance at the advertisements in any important educational magazine confirms this beyond any doubt. And however noble the motives of the industry, its products often tend to be predicated on the basis of market research rather than empirical, academic research. Secondly, there *is* a general, uninformed, and intense public panic about students' apparent lack of reading ability. A third fact — to which most classroom teachers would attest — is that a wide gap exists in most schools between the reading expert's ability to identify problems, and the classroom teacher's ability, training and facilities for dealing with them. To add to this problem, most teachers presume that reading is the exclusive responsibility of the English teacher or reading teacher. The most depressing reality of all — and a reality which the previous ones help to create — is that adolescent slower learners are generally convinced that they cannot read, a conviction which manifests itself in a variety of negative attitudes. These attitudes in turn become part of the *un-reading cycle* so characteristic of many adolescent slower learners. The cycle is an *"un"* rather than a *"non"* reading cycle, for these adolescents *can* read, but they *choose not* to, a factor based on their emotional rather than on their intellectual outlook. They are not *non*-readers therefore, but simply *un*-readers.

The un-reading cycle
(how it works)

1. The adolescent slower learner has a nagging doubt about his ability to read, and in most cases believes he cannot read up to the level that his teacher and his society expect. Therefore he avoids reading.

2. In a reading, or English, or any other class this student is presented with some reading challenge by the teacher.

3. The student avoids or withdraws from the challenge. The method is limited only to the student's ingenuity. Some sleep; others become obstreperous; others use the common ploys of asking to be excused, to sharpen a pencil, etc. Some feign illness. The bolder ones simply state with pride that they have "never read a book — ever!"

4. A crucial stage. Teacher now attempts to adjust to the problem. One or more of several options are available here.

   (a) Present simpler reading challenges. Too often these are books, or reading texts from lower grade levels. To the adolescent slower learner, the juvenile appearance of these materials is offensive. Sometimes the potential for insult is increased by materials stamped "Booster Reader" or "Simplified Series", etc.

   (b) Student is transferred to a remedial class.

   (c) A reading achievement test is administered to discover "at what level" the student is reading. Usually he does very poorly because he already feels he cannot read. Administering a test at this stage is like increasing the depth of the pool for a non-swimmer.

5. The treatment he receives *confirms* for this slower learner his doubt in his ability to read.

   Recycle

1^2. Adolescent slower learner is now certain he cannot read.

2^2. In reading, or English, or any other class . . . .

In the area of reading, more than in any other part of his education, the adolescent slower learner is a *victim*. A victim of his own self-perception, of his teachers' perceptions and expectations, and of society's panic.

Breaking the Un-Reading Cycle

Problem #1

It is interesting to consider that in spite of the great importance educators (and the world) attach to reading, it is not usually taught formally, after a student leaves elementary school (except of course for "special" programs). The essential reason is not hard to determine. Prior to the Second World War, and even for some years after, those students who couldn't, or wouldn't read, had simply left school by adolescence. Hence it was always assumed that secondary school students could and would read, and that reading instruction was unnecessary.

With today's adolescents however, far greater numbers are staying in school. Social welfare legislation, the modern *need* for education, and a stay-in-school social ethic has encouraged this. Consequently, there are enormous differences in the reading abilities and reading habits of adolescent classes, especially slower learner classes. But of one fact, any teacher of adolescent slower learners can be certain: These students can *decode*.

Because they are adolescents, they have been involved in the educational process for at least six or seven or more years. Thus even the poorest reader among them can at least read words. This ability will vary of course, but of that common denominator one can be sure. Those students with physical handicaps so severe as to be unable to decode, are usually placed in highly specialized situations before adolescence. Those with milder handicaps or those with handicaps for which the system has no provision — in short, those handicapped students who are customarily placed in adolescent slower learner classes — even these can usually decode.

Therefore, one of the initial tasks to be faced by a teacher of adolescent slower learners, is not to teach phonics, not to teach suffixes and prefixes, not to drill vocabulary, not to give dictionary exercises: in sum, the teacher of adolescent slower learners does *not* have to "return to basics", because these students already know the basics. And the negative emotional attitude toward reading, held by these students, is such that a return to basics merely intensifies the un-reading cycle. Rather, the teacher's task is to utilize the adolescent slower learner's essential grasp of basics to break the emotional un-reading cycle. The teacher's task is to help the student convince himself that he *can* do more than read words, that he can in fact, *read*. To accomplish this, is considerably simpler than most teachers — and students — believe.

Problem #2

The second major problem faced by teachers of the adolescent slower learner is infinitely more subtle. Once the students are confident of their ability to read, or have at least overcome their individual tendencies to avoid the challenge of reading, the next stage is developing a *reading habit*. Call it self-motivated reading, or willingness-to-read, or independent reading, the terminology makes little difference. What is important is that the adolescent slower learner approach the world of books *on his own*.

If there is any single factor which frustrates teachers and slower learners alike, it is the latter group's almost total ignorance of the universe contained in books. Put simply, the teachers are *in* that universe; most adolescent slower learners are *not*. And the teacher's problem of course, is how to introduce, not compel, these students to that universe. The success rate for many teachers is not high, for the counter-forces are hard to fight. Usually, teachers themselves have entered the universe of books through a set of highly conducive circumstances. Teachers tend to be middle class, where books are highly regarded. Many were read to as children, grew up with books in the home, experienced early success in reading in their schooling. Lacking these advantages, most slower learners, especially by adolescence, have not only failed to enter that universe, but have often rejected it.

Frequently that sense of rejection is intensified by poorly thought-out teaching traditions, which are successful for some students but rarely for slower learners: compulsory book reports; arbitrary visits to the library; prescribed quantities of "supplementary" reading; teaching *one* novel to a whole class at once. Nevertheless, in the universe of books lies one of the adolescent slower learner's avenues to a more positive concept of self, and no matter how impossible the task may seem, it is a teacher's responsibility to attempt to lead these students to reading.

The Needs of A Common-Sense Reading Program

1. An absolutely infallible method for turning an adolescent slower learner into a permanent un-reader is to place him in a special reading class, and then label that class *remedial,* or *compensatory,* or *opportunity,* or *special* or . . . . The reading factor, or rather un-reading factor, in a slower learner's makeup is so profoundly emotional that placing him in a group where the label clearly identifies the level of expectation, seriously erodes his confidence. By calling a student remedial, or his

program remedial, one merely assures that he will work precisely at this level, and quite possibly never go beyond it.

How to identify or categorize such a class, if one rejects the term, *remedial,* could then be a problem. But the answer does not lie in finding yet another term, for it too will quickly acquire the pejorative overtone that students sense so readily. Rather, for adolescents the answer lies in simply not having a special *reading* class at all! (Except of course, where necessary for handicapped students.)

2. If there is no special reading class, what then? Every school is likely to have a group of slower learning adolescents caught in the un-reading cycle. And it it also likely that many of these students will be in the same class. To make them the "special reading class" would probably lead to over-emphasizing the *skills* of reading with the majority of this thrust directed exclusively at comprehension practice and vocabulary drills. A common-sense reading program needs more than this, for comprehension practice and vocabulary drills by themselves have little chance of encouraging the *reading habit.* In addition to work in comprehension, there must be practice in perception, in listening, in developing oral fluency, in writing, in relating issues and concepts. And all these needs can be pursued without creating or *labelling* a special reading class. They can be taught in English class, or language arts class, or in whatever type of class structure by which the rest of the school is identified.

3. A third, and vitally necessary component of a useful reading program is some form of very careful, but not total, individualizing. That all students — especially slower learners — read at widely varying levels of speed and comprehension is so obvious a fact that it requires little elaboration. Yet how to individualize without locking a whole class into some form of pre-packaged, programmed material, is a challenge that not too many teachers have overcome.

Some pre-packaged, individualized reading programs are quite effective. But they are not enough. Nor are they likely to develop the reading habit in a student. People who read must have more stimulation than simply recording their progress on a chart, as useful as this is. Reading is a human endeavor, a human activity, and promoting it can only be accomplished on a human-to-human basis. Ultimately, individualizing must be recognized as just one more important part of a reading program for slower learners.

4. The student's conscious observation of his own successful progress is another mandatory feature of a common-sense program. A progress chart (such as mentioned in 3) is helpful for the student, but encourage-

ment and praise from his teachers is far more important. This kind of encouragement is vital in breaking the un-reading cycle, for it helps to overcome the negative aspiration of the adolescent slower learner. Schiffman*, in a study of eighty-four adolescent slower learners, found that 78 per cent had average intelligence scores on either the Verbal or Performance scales of the WISC, and that 39 per cent had average scores on both. Yet only 14 per cent of the pupils themselves felt they had average ability — and only 7 per cent of their teachers held this view!

5. A further need is implied in a statement once made to me by Andrew (see p. 10):

> "When are we gonna' stop readin' *reading,* and start readin' *something?"*

Andrew, along with a lot of other adolescent slower learners regards the verb *read,* as transitive. To him, practice reading materials are devices for "dummy runs". Reading, for Andrew and other slower learners must have a purpose. It must lead to something — a problem to be solved, a short assignment to be completed, or, simply something to be enjoyed.

6. *Every* teacher of the adolescent slower learner is a teacher of reading. Generally, teachers of mathematics and sciences expect too much of those who supposedly bear the responsibility for reading instruction. Subject specialists must necessarily contribute to any reading program, simply because the "reading teacher" often cannot cope with special languages. For example, present the following passage to any group of teachers whose area of concentration is literature, or language study. Ask them what it means and then request a paraphrase, in their own words.

> ABC is an equilateral triangle, and PQR are points on the sides BC, AC, AB respectively such that PB is congruent to CQ is congruent to AR. If P is not the midpoint of BC then the segments AP, BQ, and CR intersect in the vertices of the triangle XYZ. Prove that triangle XYZ is equilateral.†

7. The final need of a common-sense reading program for adolescent slower learners, is one that, if fulfilled, would likely preclude any other

---

* G. B. Schiffman, "An Interdisciplinary Approach to the Identification and Remediation of Severe Reading Disabilities," *Junior College and Adult Reading Program* (Milwaukee: National Reading Conference, 1967) pp. 14-26.

† J. J. Del Grande, and J. C. Egsgard, *Mathematics II,* 2nd edition (Toronto: Gage, 1969).

requirement: namely, an understanding, perceptive, common-sense teacher!

A teacher who is capable of regarding reading achievement tests and reading machines with informed, critical perspective, a teacher who uses the material of a reading program with the students, and not the material itself uppermost in mind, a teacher who understands the adolescent slower learner's negative aspirations and consequent avoidance techniques, a teacher who is willing to forego discussions in literary criticism for techniques which encourage slower learners to read *anything,* no matter what the "literary value" — that is a teacher who will break the un-reading cycle.

A Practical Approach

Getting Adolescent Slower Learners to Read — and Keeping Them At It

NOTE: For any teacher who may consider implementing the following program, there are three important factors to consider.

1. The program aims specifically at breaking the un-reading cycle. Its objective is to get slower learners out of the program and into the universe of books as quickly as possible. Because Step One begins at the lowest common denominator for adolescents, letter recognition and word formation, some teachers may feel it unnecessary to begin at this point; the program therefore is designed such that teachers may begin anywhere in the series of steps, and where appropriate may skip certain steps, or even reverse the order of some steps.

2. Each step or level presents sample exercises. The amount of work deemed necessary at each level is, of course, up to the teacher. If more work at a particular stage is desirable, then preparation of further exercises is a necessary, but simple, task.

3. The steps *must* be pursued individually and without competition. Each student works up the scale at his own speed, and proceeds from step to step at his own pace, guided by the teacher.

Step One: *letter recognition and word formation*

The purpose of this exercise is to deal with the many adolescent slower learners who have made the conscious but emotional decision *not* to read. The exercise, therefore, merely involves playing the game. (Any exercise, similar to that given here, would suffice. The example in Step One has been named by former un-readers as the most interesting.)

Students are presented with one or several of the following faces, each of which is made up of letters that form a name. For example, the following face-names, in order, are PEGGY, PETER, SYLVIA, EDWARD*. Simply present them to the students, *each with his own copy*. Experience indicates that exercises like these are appealing to even the most negative slower learners. The same is true of Step Two.

Step Two: *further word recognition, with additional complications*

Note that this second step is only slightly more involved than the first. This exercise should be presented to students *with* written instructions, as follows, but the teacher should read them aloud.

Word Searches

1. Look for the words from the Word List, in the diagram of letters. Find them by reading FORWARD, BACKWARD, UP, DOWN, and DIAGONALLY. The words are always in a straight line and they never skip letters.

---

* An excellent source of these puzzles is N. G. Pulsford, *4th Junior Puzzle Book* (London: Pan, 1958).

2. Draw a circle around the word in the diagram once you've found it and cross it off the Word List. Words overlap and letters are used more than once. However, you will never use up all the diagram.

Variations of Step Two are possible, and often desirable. The puzzles can be designed simpler than what appears here, by having all the words horizontal, and reading from left to right. Or the search can be complicated by presenting a diagram *without* a word list. (In this situation, be certain that the subject of the diagram is a familiar one to the students, perhaps place names from the local area.) Also, students can design puzzles for their classmates — a challenging and useful exercise, and one that they do well.

If you're a person who likes to build things, you may have worked with some of the 36 building materials listed on the opposite page. You'll find them all hidden in the diagram below.*

Diagram

C	O	N	C	R	E	T	E	C	L	A	Y	B	T
G	L	O	S	S	S	N	O	W	E	C	V	W	L
N	M	G	D	E	R	G	O	O	E	M	I	Q	P
L	O	E	A	H	E	O	O	T	T	G	E	S	R
L	E	R	K	C	D	B	I	I	S	X	L	N	E
R	T	L	I	N	M	N	M	M	H	A	L	P	T
H	R	A	B	A	A	N	D	B	T	C	I	S	S
H	E	T	B	R	O	N	Z	E	B	L	T	T	A
K	P	H	G	B	A	X	M	R	E	R	I	I	L
C	P	E	J	S	M	M	I	S	A	C	L	M	P
O	O	S	T	U	C	C	O	W	K	T	E	B	E
R	C	Y	D	Z	K	O	T	S	B	L	P	Q	C

* *Word Search Puzzles,* third book (New York: Dell, 1972), pp. 10, 11.

Word List

1. Bamboo
2. Branches
3. Brick
4. Bronze
5. Cement
6. Clay
7. Concrete
8. Copper
9. Earth
10. Granite
11. Ice
12. Iron
13. Lathes
14. Lime
15. Logs
16. Marble
17. Metal
18. Mud

19. Piles   (*supporting posts*)
20. Pitch
21. Plaster
22. Reeds
23. Rock
24. Sand
25. Slate
26. Snow
27. Steel
28. Sticks
29. Stone
30. Straw
31. Stucco
32. Tar
33. Tile
34. Timber
35. Twigs
36. Wood

Answers

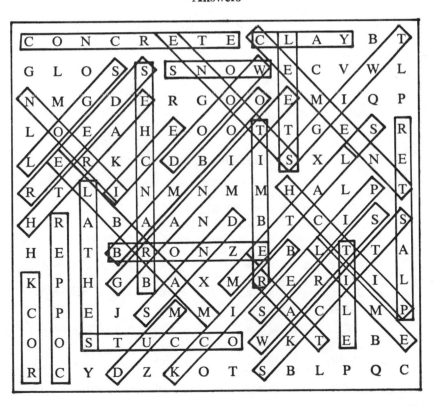

Yes, They Can!

Step Three: *leading from words to sentences*

By this stage, the vast majority of un-readers will have been reading words with varying degrees of success (and success is the operative word). The transfer from words to sentences is a relatively simple accomplishment in the context of gaming or problem-solving that has already been established. Here are three sample exercises. These again, can be presented in any number of altered forms, with varying degrees of difficulty, according to the teacher's wishes.

At the teacher's discretion, these exercises might be presented to the students without any comment other than: "The instructions are on the sheet." Most students will read them on their own.

Find the Jewels

In each sentence, a jewel is hidden. Find the jewel and circle it. The jewels are listed below in order. Number one is done for you.

1. Do not [rub y]our eyes.
2. In countries such as Cambodia, Monday is a day of rest.
3. You will see a gate down by the road.
4. The next clue is hidden in a pear lying under the tree.
5. The horse will gallop all the way home.

1. ruby
2. diamond
3. agate
4. pearl
5. opal

Find the Animals

1. Try [to ad]d all the costs first, before you make any decisions.
2. He made Eric aware of all the facts first.
3. Millie came late to work again.
4. I would rather stay here with my friends.
5. Florence Nightingale is a famous English nurse.
6. One day she will be a very great actress.
7. The revised schedule says that the train will now go at 5:30 p.m.
8. Don't slam both those doors when you leave!
9. There were pigeons nesting throughout the abandoned house.
10. Marc owes me ten dollars.

1. toad	6. beaver
2. deer	7. goat
3. camel	8. lamb
4. rat	9. ewe - pig
5. mouse	10. cow

Names, Please*

In each sentence, a 4-letter name is hidden, just as 'KATE' is hidden in: The boy lost his sKATEs.

1. Pat, of course, is an Irish name.
2. Number one comes before number two.
3. Father did all the decorating.
4. Going to a lecture is not much fun.
5. She took part in all the school games.
6. Many a boy doesn't like his parents to hug him.
7. Manners maketh the man.
8. Cotton is often wound on reels.
9. One should always tell the truth.
10. To run the mile in four minutes is not easy.
11. There are many different Army ranks.
12. Usually the guard travels in the van.
13. Every girl likes to be adorable.
14. All car lights should be on after dark.
15. Having no racket, you can't play tennis.
16. A tight-rope walker should never lose his balance.

The Names: (They are scrambled!)
Otto - Dora - Nora - Iris - Ruth - Hugh - Anne - Olga - Alec -
Evan - Alan - Emil - Carl - Cora - Myra - Bert.

Step Four: *transferring from single sentences to continuous prose*

A significant difference between Steps Three and Four is that in the latter stage, multiple information must be retained and inter-related — in other words: reading.

The point of Step Four is only that students amass the information necessary to solve the mystery. The solution itself is unimportant, although it can add excitement to the exercise. Only two samples follow, but this type of exercise is relatively easy for any teacher to design.

Creative Mystery

CLUE #1:   JIM AND JEAN ARE DEAD.

To find clue #2, change the words in the following sentence around, so that it makes sense.

CLUE #2:   LYING ARE JEAN AND JIM FLOOR THE ON.

To find clue #3, change the order of the letters in each word in the following sentence.

CLUE #3:   ETH ORFLO SI ETW.

---

* Pulford, *4th Junior Puzzle Book.*

To find clue #4, cross out every third letter.

CLUE #4: THWERVE IJS BAROSKEAN GOLAQSS VON RTHBE FALOAOR

To find clue #5, read the sentence backwards.

CLUE #5: ROOM THE IN TABLE A IS THERE.

To find clue #6, read each word in the sentence (but not the sentence itself) backwards.

CLUE #6: EHT HTOLCELBAT SI GNILLAF FFO.

To find clue #7, separate the following into a sentence which has seven words.

CLUE #7: THEREISADOGINTHEROOM.

BONUS
CLUE: NAMUH TON ERA NAEJ DNA MIJ.

QUESTION: Who are Jim and Jean? How did they die?*

Creative Mystery

CLUE #1: A MAN IS LYING FACE DOWNWARD.

To find clue #2, read the next sentence backwards.

CLUE #2: AROUND ELSE ONE NO IS THERE.

To find clue #3, cross out the letter R wherever you see it in the next sentence.

CLUE #3: THRER RPRRLARCRE RIRS RAR RBRIRG RFIRERLDR.

To find clue #4, move the second letter in each word to its right place.

CLUE #4: HTE AMN SI EDAD.

To find clue #5, read each word in the sentence, (but not the sentence itself) backward.

CLUE #5: NO SIH KCAB EREHT SI A KCAP.

---

* They are tropical fish. The dog pulled them off the table.

To find clue #6, divide the following into a sentence having six words.

CLUE #6:   THEREISSOMETHINGINTHEPACK.

BONUS
CLUE: Each letter in the following words is advanced by one in the alphabet. For example, IF, is actually HE.

IF JT XFBSJOH B NJMJUBSZ VOJGPSN.

QUESTION: What happened to the man?

The variety of activities possible at this stage is limited only to the number of ideas generated by teachers and students. Students can develop very simple codes. Write a short message in the code, and then exchange to "crack" the code.* Students can cut headlines out of newspapers. Put parts of them together to make new statements.

But such exercises have value only as long as they are useful in breaking the un-reading cycle. For a class to spend a very long time on any one of these exercises might be a mistake. On the other hand, some classes may benefit from more extended work at this level. Experience shows, however, that all classes of slower learners, whether they have generally broken out of the un-reading cycle or not, enjoy a return to some of these exercises on an intermittent basis.

Step Five: *further, but more involved, practice with continuous prose*
Take a short comic strip story and cut it into its component frames. Label each frame A, B, C, etc., and arrange them in a confused order. The object is for the student to rearrange them in an appropriate order, by reading the balloon captions and determining the most logical and coherent sequence.

The visual aspect of comic strips helps students accomplish this task with relatively little difficulty. A slight complication can be added by doing the same exercise with a coherent prose article, newspaper story, or piece of short fiction.

Step Six: *dealing with multiple information in continuous prose, drawing out an abstract idea, or concept*

This step involves even more complicated reading and problem solving, but the step is made easier by having students work in pairs, cooperating

---

* See H. S. Zim, *Codes and Secret Writing* (New York: Scholastic Book Services, 1960.)

toward a solution. Note that the exercise below is stated in the simplest possible terms. Students must *read* the instructions, *determine* the object of the game, and *discover* how to play it. At the teacher's discretion, the instructions can be re-stated in more complex terms, if this is desirable.

The Pick-Up Game

Place sixteen sticks in *four* rows of *one, three, five* and *seven*.

Players take turns removing as many sticks as they wish, from any *one* row.

The object is to force your opponent to take the very last stick.

The second example, although a simpler exercise in principle, is more complicated to explain. Consequently, the degree of reading and abstraction required, is greater. Nevertheless, it is important that students do the reading and thinking on their own. Ideally, the teacher will do nothing other than act as an interested observer or occasionally be the arbiter of a dispute.

Filling the Squares

• • • • • • •

• • • • • • •

• • • • • • •

• • • • • • •

• • • • • • •

• • • • • • •

• • • • • • •

Each player takes a turn drawing a *horizontal* or *vertical* line, between *any two adjacent* dots. A player may draw a line anywhere on the board. The player who closes a square, puts his initial in that square. When a player closes a square, he gets another turn, right away, before his opponent does. Whoever has more initials when all the squares are drawn, wins the game.

Filling the Squares

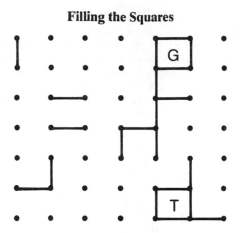

Step Seven: *transferring to longer continuous prose; increasing the verbal fluency/listening factor*

One of the features of the *reading habit* — that is, one of the pleasures enjoyed by those who have met the universe of books — is sharing experiences in reading. Whether by direct reference to a book, or by the sharing of an experience implied in a book, readers enjoy with one another, that kind of mutual, abstract excursion which un-readers never understand or appreciate. Therefore it is necessary to build into any adolescent slower learner reading program, this kind of shared experience, by encouraging discussions related to the pieces being read.

Such a feature must be introduced *early* in a reading program; hence a major part of the previous Step Six, and now, Step Seven, is oral, allowing for participation in a shared experience. (And oral work is built into the subsequent steps of the program.)

Note also, that the vocabulary of the piece in Step Seven is reasonably difficult. This is quite deliberate, and is designed as part of the attack on the un-reading cycle. As any teacher of the adolescent slower learner knows, a common avoidance technique these students employ, is closing a book with an "I can't" as soon as the first polysyllabic word appears. Somewhere along the way, therefore, students must meet, and overcome "big" words. Ideally this should take place at a point in the program when frequent student-teacher contact is possible.

Some teachers may choose to read the following example aloud to their students, and even do a demonstration, before turning the students to work, in pairs. The degree of structure is, as always, up to the individual teacher.

Palmistry

Another predictive system said to have existed as far back as 3000
B.C. in China, is the art of palmistry. This method of telling the
future of an individual lies in examining the palm of his hand. His
mental or moral disposition is associated with the various irre-
gularities and flexion folds of the skin. Although palmistry is
considered by many people to be unscientific and without basis
in fact, the case of the famous Mrs. Jeane Dixon does cause
second thought. At the age of eight, Mrs. Dixon's palm was read
by a gypsy woman who proclaimed, "This child has the gift of
prophecy."

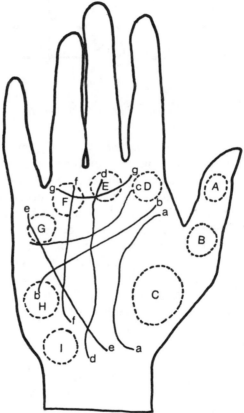

*(Over one hundred interpretations have been recorded in the
art of palmistry; the one that follows is fairly simplified.)*

Each of the capital letters denotes an area of the palm where
the flesh rises in a "mountain." The size of the particular mountain
usually correlates directly with the particular quality of the person.
"A" for example, denotes *will,* and if the individual has a high
"A" mountain, he will have considerable will power. A low mountain would therefore denote weakness or a lack of will.

B—logic; C—(mount of Venus) charity and love; D—(mount of Jupiter) religiosity, ambition, love of honor, pride; E—(mount of Saturn) wisdom, good fortune, prudence (when Saturn is small it denotes ignorance and failure.); F—(mount of Apollo) success, celebrity, intelligence; G—(mount of Mercury) love of knowledge, industry; H—(mount of Mars) courage, resolution; I—(mound of the Moon) sensitiveness, morality, good conduct; aa—life line; bb—line of the head; cc—line of the heart; dd—line of fate; ee—line of the liver; ff—line of fortune; gg—ring of Venus.

(Note that the topography of the hand can be seen most easily, by letting the fingers relax while slightly apart, then closing them.)

Analyze your own hand and someone else's hand. Compare your results with others in your group. Is there any correlation between your reading, and what you know about yourself?

Step Eight: *perceiving specific details in a piece of longer continuous prose*

The idea inherent in the following passage is self-explanatory. Step Eight is another stage in the *gradual* transfer of the slower learner from un-reading to reading.

The Case of the Strange Suicide

Inspector Bower braked hard as he pulled up in front of the big office building. Ahead of him a patrol car sat, flashing its red message. The white door stood open, an indication of how fast the driver had responded to the emergency call.

Bower pressed through the crowd that had gathered on the sidewalk. There is nothing to see, he said to himself, but crowds gather anyway. All you need to do is turn on your red light, and you've got people all over the place. And they all want to see blood too!

"They're up there!" a doorman was shouting at him.

"Who's up there?" Bower wanted to know.

"Your uniformed man, and the guy who turned on the alarm! He saw it all y'know! He saw the guy kill himself!" The doorman was very excited.

Bower looked around the lobby. "Where's the elevator?" he asked.

"It's broken!" the doorman said. "You'll have to use the stairs. Fourth floor. The door's right over there."

Inspector Bower was puffing by the time he made it up to the murder scene. The patrolman was standing in the doorway with a tall man in a chauffeur's uniform.

"Right this way, Inspector!" said the patrolman. "The body's

95

still there. We haven't touched a thing." He pointed to the chauffeur. "This man is a witness. Saw the guy hang himself."

The office was big. And it was rich. The furniture was expensive, the rug was thick. There was a bar set into one wall. In fact, Bower thought, the only thing wrong was the body of a middle-aged man, a rope around his neck, hanging from the ceiling. Beneath him, an upturned footstool lay on the rug.

Bower walked over to the window, pulled the drapes and looked out. The crowd was still there and getting larger. Two more police cars had come in and added to the excitement. He turned to the chauffeur.

"You're the witness, eh? Do you know the dead man?"

"Well sure. He's — was — my boss! I was coming to pick him up. That's the limousine out in front. The grey one."

Inspector Bower looked at him carefully. "Tell us what happened."

"Well, I just pulled up in front and got out. The boss always limped a bit, see, and I was going to help him down the stairs. When I got out of the car, I looked up. I always do 'cause sometimes he waits on the balcony. He gets mad if I'm late. Anyway, I looked up, see, and there he is getting up on that footstool with the rope around his neck. And I know he's going to kill himself, see, but with the elevator broken, by the time I ran up four floors, he was dead already, see?"

"Yes I see," said Bower. "I think you'd better come with me. You've got more to tell us."

What made Inspector Bower suspicious?*

A variation of Step Eight is possible by having the students write mysteries for their classmates to solve. A teacher can be very helpful here, by providing clues which may be the focus of a mystery. The students then write a mystery around the particular clue. Here is a sample, written by one of my students. Before publication here, it was of course, very carefully reworked and rewritten by the student, whose clue incidentally, is built around a hot versus a cold, automobile engine.

A policeman suddenly came upon two cars headed in opposite directions and parked opposite each other on the sides of the road. Between them was a man who had been killed a few minutes before by one of them. Each driver said that the other had killed the man. Mr. A said that he, for the past two hours, had been examining the stones in a cemetery which was nearby, and that he had just returned to find the accident. Mr. B claimed, that as he approached the spot, he had seen Mr. A's car strike the man, and that he had stopped to help. There were no witnesses; and,

---

* The drapes in the office were closed.

the policeman could tell nothing from marks on the ground, or the position of the body. After a brief investigation however, he definitely proved Mr. B. guilty.

How did the policeman arrive at this conclusion?

Step Nine: *reading for a purpose*

This is the final step before moving to full length books. It is an important step for a number of reasons. In the first place, the adolescent slower learner often reacts negatively to reading when he is faced with one book of continuous prose (e.g. a novel); the thought of reading a whole book is often more than he feels he can do. Therefore, passages like the following one, *long* but not a whole book, help him make that step.

Secondly, passages like the following help make the transfer out of gaming, and at the same time accommodate Andrew's requirement that "we must read *something,* not just read *reading.*"

Thirdly, the passage is from the same book which had the palmistry exercise in it. In other words, the book is familiar. And perhaps even more important, any book which looks less formidable because it is broken up into pieces of varying length — broken up in terms of content, and broken up visually — helps the adolescent slower learner to transfer to full length books. Transfer from a collection of prose articles to books, is much easier and more natural for any student than transferring from a machine, or from cards, or from a special "reading book".

Why We Split Up

The Smiths

His Side

I'm a quiet-living, commonplace sort of guy. I would have been quite happy living the rest of my life in my hometown, being with my childhood friends, running my father's business.

Now I'm a divorced man (I cringe everytime I have to put that on an application form), living in the big city (I could never live my divorce down in that town) and I'm going with a nice-enough girl that I'll probably never marry for fear of another failure.

Avoidable? Sure it was. But when you confront stubborn young teen-agers with pigheaded parents (hers), you're bound to get trouble.

They knew from the start that it was a bad match but it seemed to me for the wrong reasons. They were plain prejudiced about my being a Catholic, they didn't like my working for my father, a garage-owner, nor our comparatively humble way of life. In a word, I wasn't good enough for her. Nobody was asking whether she was good for me, by the way.

So what did they do? They gave her more rules, more discipline (it wasn't uncommon for Isabel to have welts from her father's strap), more responsibilities at home. Looking back it was no wonder she turned to me for love and understanding.

Finally, it got so bad that we decided to get married secretly, just to get them off our backs. We were both eighteen — she quit grade thirteen and I continued working for Dad.

Married life was very pleasant. Sex was beautiful (it's funny, even now she admits I'm the only man who ever really satisfied her). I guess Isabel had a lot of time on her hands (because of my father's business, she could have a car any time she wanted and I thought that should keep her happy). By the end of the first year, she was pretty determined that I should finish off my high school and get to university. Well, that was all right by me, but from then on we were only marking time until the split.

By then she had met that man — the fiancé of her best friend. She was dazzled by him. He was quite a guy all right — even I had to like him. When we moved to the big city we saw a lot of him and his girl friend. I wasn't thinking in terms of the possibility of Isabel being unfaithful, but I compared myself with that man and knew no matter how much book-crashing I did, I wouldn't be in his class.

The marriage was skidding on thin ice. I was under a lot of pressure at school, money was really tight and I had to do all the housework (she always was a terrible housecleaner) and in my spare time I was overhauling her sports car. I thought all this was responsible for the strain, that I had probably been too much of a slave to her. Finally at the end of the summer (I had failed my French), I decided to go back north to give my father a hand, and leave her on her own for awhile, maybe make her a little lonesome. Well, I came back unexpectedly one weekend and found her in bed with him. And so, after two years of marriage, I sued for divorce.

It took me two years to get over the dismal failure of it all. Now there's this girl — really nice. I think I love her, I keep telling myself I'm not afraid, but I don't know.

One single thing sticks in my mind. Parents could do a lot to avoid this kind of mess, simply by letting things run their natural course. Without her parents' opposition, we wouldn't have had anything to talk about in the first place.

Her Side

My husband flunked out of marriage. I mean, I think I would have stuck around if he had got high-enough grades to go on in university. I would have stuck it even though by then I knew that his IQ was thirty points lower than mine.

I married Tom for all the wrong reasons. First, there was my family situation. A stepmother I despised (my parents were divorced) and an over-bearing strict father. Other girls had freedom. I was allowed out once a week until midnight, and everyday my bed was checked to see if it were properly made. There were heavy baby-sitting responsibilities with my stepsister and stepbrother.

My father is a businessman and we lived up to a fairly high standard. I despised the materialism of our homelife and wanted to go to university and eventually become a writer. But my stepmother convinced me I would never be more than a stenographer; so I co-operated beautifully and had to repeat grade twelve.

In the meantime, I started to go out with Tom. He was big and strong and protective and spelled escape in capital letters. We went steady through my two years in grade twelve and finally decided to get married — secretly.

My father had no use for Tom. Tom's dad was also in business, but there the similarity ended. Tom's family, including Tom were all devout Catholics; we were fairly casual Anglicans. As I said, we had this fairly high standard of living whereas Tom's father took home $75 a week.

It wasn't that business was bad. Tom once boasted that his father had salted away $40,000 in the bank. See what I mean. They weren't spending it, they weren't investing it in the business, just hoarding it.

There was a certain dumb, slow acceptance of things in the way Tom's family lived. Generation after generation of them had lived the same way, married nice girls in the town and not one of them had ever ventured away.

Dad said once that my marrying Tom was like putting a racehorse with a cart horse. I knew the difference between us all right. After two years of going steady, there was very little I didn't know about Tom.

Except sex. Tom and I were terribly attracted to each other, but both had backgrounds that forbade us to do anything about it. He would not go against his religious upbringing.

We were to get married secretly, but two weeks before the wedding my father found out. He offered Tom and me a thousand dollars to go anywhere in the world to shack up for a while and get it over with.

Had that not shocked me so completely and had I been able to accept my father's offer, the whole disaster of marriage and divorce would have been avoided. I know that now. But at the time, my whole world was shattered. My father, the ultimate hypocrite; there wasn't one value I could look on without confusion. I fled all the faster to Tom's arms.

We lived in the town for a year. I did nothing but keep house (I use the expression loosely) and Tom brought home his seventy dollars a week. Slowly I began to see the dimensions of the nightmare I had signed myself up for. By the end of that year, I was a screaming shrew and poor Tom was finally nagged into pulling out of his father's business.

I didn't care what it was, but it had to be a degree of some kind, a profession, a breakaway from the dull old past. I was willing to work and pay the whole shot. Tom finally agreed.

Two things happened at the end of that year. He took aptitude tests to find out which direction he should take. Well, his IQ was 115 and he was told he should take his grade thirteen, concentrate in maths, head for a small university and take engineering.

Well, that was still all right. I said to myself. We'll make it on those terms and be happy. I got a job in Toronto taking home sixty-four dollars a week, and Tom started on his grade thirteen.

By then, I had also met Howard, fiancé of my best friend in our hometown.

Howard was a dashing sort of figure. Brilliant, sure of himself, handsome, well on his way in the stock market in Toronto.

We clicked right away. When Tom and I moved to Toronto, we saw a lot of Howard and Carol. At first it was an exhilarating meeting of two very fast minds, but an affair was inevitable. By the time it started, I knew my marriage was hopeless, that Tom would never be the man I would respect. And, of course, he didn't make his thirteen. It went on for several months before Tom discovered us and he sued for divorce. I felt relieved.

The affair ended eventually. Howard said we had everything except love on his part. Where am I now? Living with a divorced man who says he's past the love-and-marriage thing now. I don't know . . . I'm still looking for it.

1. Although the Smiths must share the blame for the failure of their marriage, do you feel that one is more to blame than the other?

2. Examine carefully the way each account is written. How can you tell from the choice of words, the kind of detail, and the personal point of view that the Smiths were very different personalities?

Step Ten: *novels on a theme*

By this point, if the stages have been followed carefully, and if the students have been encouraged and helped by a teacher with genuine empathy, any unhandicapped slower learner will be ready for a full length book. However, one factor of overwhelming importance still remains: *not all the students in the class read with the same ability, and they are not therefore, all ready for the same book.* Step Ten then, is designed to allow each student to read a book, the difficulty of which is within the approximate range of his ability.

Thus Step Ten is individualized, but still one more feature is necessary. In order to provide motivation, atmosphere, the factor of shared experience, the security of the class unit, and the opportunity for frequent student-teacher contact, Step Ten is built on a common theme in which all can participate. The theme provides a basic motif on which to build a variety of mutual activities. Each student in the class therefore, reads at his own ability/interest level, but remains a part of the class unit as it works toward a common objective.

Theme: Know Thyself

The list of possible themes is very long. The example provided here was nominated by three different classes of adolescent slower learners, as the most popular. Also, the materials are not necessarily limited to those itemized here.

Materials

1. Film: *Nahanni* (col., 18 min. 24 sec. National Film Board of Canada) or *any* film which is likely to stimulate interest in whatever it is that makes people strive for elusive goals.

2. Basis for oral discussion, writing projects and panel discussions: *Prose of Relevance I,* Methuen Publications.
   Some passages are included in the following pages.

3. Novels: The following are of mature interest but of varied difficulty and length. Two or three copies of each title should be made available to the class.
   (a) Swinburn: *Angelita Nobody*
   (McGraw-Hill-City Limits Series) very easy reading
   (b) Halliburton: *Cry, Baby!*
   (McGraw-Hill-City Limits Series) very easy reading
   (c) Brodsky: *Cutting Out*
   (McGraw-Hill-City Limits Series) slightly more difficult than (a) and (b)
   (d) Tate: *Sam and Me*
   (Macmillan — Topliner Series) easy reading
   (e) Leach: *Answering Miss Roberts*
   (Macmillan — Topliner Series) a little more difficult than (d)
   (f) Davis: *Anything For A Friend* (Bantam, paperback) not difficult reading, breezy style
   (g) Ruben: *Jordi/Lisa and David* (Ballantine, paperback) non-fiction but fascinating, not too difficult but more involved than the Topliners
   (h) Axline: *Dibs: In Search of Self* (Ballantine, paperback) a little more involved than (g)
   (i) McKay: *Dave's Song* (Bantam, paperback) not difficult, of great interest
   (j) Other novels which always work well are:
   Catcher in the Rye and *Of Mice and Men.*

Suggested Procedure

First Day: A viewing of *Nahanni* and discussion based on the main character's motivation and goals.

Second Day: Discuss the quotations from Browning and Alcoholics Anonymous.

> . . . a man's reach should exceed his grasp,
> Or what's a heaven for?
>
> Robert Browning

> God grant me the serenity
> to accept the things I cannot change,
> Courage to change the things I can,
> And wisdom to know the difference.
>
> Alcoholics Anonymous

1. Are these two declarations incompatible?
2. (a) Which one is more appealing to you?
   (b) Does your choice reveal anything about you?
3. Exactly what are one's *values?*

At the appropriate point in the discussion present the various novels. Leave enough time for students to make their own choice and to begin reading so that they can get started on the novels of their choice; also leave time to help a student select another novel if he feels his first choice is inappropriate. You may wish to use the "Cloze" procedure described at the end of this unit.

Third Day: Silent reading during class. Discuss novels with individual students if they are willing.

Fourth Day: (Repeat third day)

Fifth Day: Introduce the passages that follow about the skier, Anne Frank, and Sheila's poem for discussion. Leave enough time for some reading at the end of the class session.

Skier to Take on Everest

KATMANDU, Nepal — (Reuters) — A leading Japanese professional skier left here yesterday for an attempt at skiing down Mount Everest from a point only 173 feet below the summit.

Yiuchiro Miura plans to ski down the world's highest mountain from 28,855 feet. Everest is 29,028 feet high.

Miura, 37, said there is only a 50-50 chance of success in the first part of the run — from the south summit to the 26,240 foot south col.

This is because of strong winds, a steep slope and rock outcroppings, he said.

He would not specify odds for the following run down from the south col into the western valley.

Miura, who will make his attempt toward the end of next month with the assistance of a 32-man Japanese expedition, said he realized that Everest's extreme altitudes, despite his oxygen supply, could seriously affect his ability to make split-second decisions and control his movements.

Miura, who will carry three stabilizing parachutes, calculates that six seconds after starting the descent from the south col he will reach the steepest stretch — an eighth of a mile of 40-degree slope.

He estimates that by this time he will be moving at 112 mph. To stop going over this speed he plans to pull one parachute ripcord five seconds after leaving the col.

He said that if the parachute does not slow him down he would be travelling at more than 125 mph. by the seventh second.

His own fastest speed is 107 mph., reached on the Matterhorn in 1964.

1. Why would someone want to do this?
2. Is there any difference between this event, and a sport like sky-diving, or even the Olympic marathon?
3. Describe some feat that you would like to perform. If your proposed adventure is dangerous, include in your description what precautions you would take.

The Diary of Anne Frank (May 3, 1944)

I am young and I possess many buried qualities; I am young and strong and am living a great adventure; I am still in the midst of it and can't grumble the whole day long. I have been given a lot, a happy nature, a great deal of cheerfulness and strength. Every day I feel that I am developing inwardly, that the liberation is drawing nearer and how beautiful nature is, how good the people are about me, how interesting this adventure is! Why, then, should I be in despair?

Anne Frank

Have you ever felt the same way as Anne Frank? Why?

Not Mine
So you
want
to know
why
I
dig pot?

Because
This world ain't mine man!
I didn't make it,
I can't change it,
I want out of it.

Sheila, aged 15.

1. Is Sheila's attitude immoral? Is it logical?
2. Write a response to Sheila's poem, as Anne Frank might have written it, or as Yiuchiro Miura (the skier) might write it.

Sixth Day: Silent reading during class.

Seventh Day: Introduce for discussion, "On Being Fifteen."

On Being Fifteen

I think the only thing that I can say about myself *for sure,* is that I'm all mixed up.

Take God for instance. Some of my friends say He doesn't exist. "Look around," they say, "where do you see any proof of God?" But they never say what to look for. And the funny thing is — I think I believe in God, but I don't know what to look for either!

Then there's necking. I lost a boyfriend because my views didn't agree with his. Some of my girlfriends go pretty far, and he thought I should too. Oh, I don't mind losing him if that's the way he thinks; but what really bugs me is that for a while I really wanted to even though I didn't. I wonder if wanting to do something is just as bad as doing it?

It wasn't quite the same with smoking pot. I didn't want to do that either but I did, because my friends were all doing it.

My parents don't help with any of this either. They never understand my feelings and I can never explain. Here I am, fifteen years old, and I think I was more certain of things when I was *ten*!

Linda, aged 15.
Prose of Relevance 1, p. 47.

1. Why are one's values clearer at ten than at fifteen?
2. Is Linda a fairly average teenager?

Eighth Day: Announce this as the last day of "in-class" reading and that a form of brief written assignment on the novel will be evaluated. (Note that some students will be on their second novel by now.)

Ninth Day: Sample assignment, to be done in class.
Select one (or two) of the questions below, and assuming the role of the main character in the novel you have read, answer as you think he or she would.

1. "When a man and woman marry, the values adopted by the new family are almost always those of the woman." Do you agree?

2. How much can you learn about a person by the way he or she dresses?

3. If you had the opportunity to take a very powerful potion that would greatly increase one of your powers *permanently,* would you take it? If you could choose the power to be increased, what one would you pick?

4. If no one cared at all about your behavior, would it change?

5. Give your description of happiness (a good chance for poetry).

Examine each of the following statements and express your reaction to them.

1. "Though mothers and fathers give us life, it is money alone which preserves it."
   Ihara Saikaku (d. 1693)

2. "A good reputation is more valuable than money."
   Publius Syrus (c. 76 B.C.)

3. "Make money, money by fair means if you can, if not, by any means money."
   Horace (d. 8 B.C.)

4. "Money: there's nothing in the world so demoralizing as money."
   Sophocles (d. 405 B.C.)

5. "The holy passion of Friendship is of so sweet and steady and loyal and enduring a nature that it will endure a lifetime, if not asked to lend money."
   Mark Twain (d. 1910)

Tenth Day: Panel discussion (an optional stage). Select several students to participate in a spontaneous panel, discussing a question which would relate to the theme of the novels they have read.

Sample Problems for Panel Discussion

Each of the following situations calls for a response that will be guided by your own personal set of values.

Situation #1

You have been employed as a lab technician working in top secret chemical warfare experiments. Inadvertently you contaminate yourself with a germ and become a carrier of a slow-working but fatal disease that is so contagious that if anyone learns of your condition you will be put in isolation until you die. There is a possible cure, but it must be performed in Tokyo and you are now in Montreal. What do you do?

Situation #2

You are the coach of a hockey team in a city where racial integration is just getting under way. There is one position to fill on your team. Of the two people who try out, one is white; his family is well-to-do; he has already been scouted by the National Hockey League and is clearly the better of the two. The second tryout is a black person; he is not as good as the white boy, but his family is poor and he would benefit from the experience with your team. You have an opportunity now, to show the city where sports people stand on the subject of integration. Your team knows that with the right person, this year they can win the championship. What do you do?

Situation #3

You and your best friend apply for summer jobs. You both want jobs badly and apply at a place where an advertisement asked for two students. The potential employer says to both of you that there has been a change in plans and now he can hire only one student. But he adds that since you were both so well qualified, he could accept either one of you. He asks the two of you to make a decision. What do you do?

Eleventh Day: Return assignments, allowing time for discussion.

Twelfth Day: Depending upon the teacher's assessment of the situation, encourage all to read one more novel beginning right away, and allow time in class for this.

The Cloze Procedure (very simplified)

For Evaluating Readability

The cloze procedure can be used to determine the appropriateness of a particular book for a particular group of students in terms of its readability. The procedure is as follows:

1. From the book in question select a passage of at least 500 words of continuous prose which the students have not yet encountered.

2. Type the passage (double spaced), putting a blank in place of every 5th word.

3. Ask the class to fill in the blanks with the missing words.

4. Score the responses, counting only exact words substituted. (Accept mis-spelling if you are sure of the word intended.)

The book in question is appropriate for any student who scores at least 44% and not above 70%. (Massive research conducted by Bormuth indicates that students learn more effectively from books in which they score between 44% and 70%.)

Maintaining the Reading Habit

Returning to the original premise that an adolescent slower learner *can* read, physical handicaps excepted, most students by this stage will be on the brink of entering the universe of books. Some, but not many, will have already moved into it. Whether or not the majority now do, is beyond any kind of specific reading program no matter how divinely inspired it may be. Whether or not the majority develop the reading habit is now up to all teachers, the parents, and the general atmosphere of both the school community, and the community at large.

In the classroom, a repetition of step ten using a different theme, is almost always successful. Intermittent returns to the earlier stages of the program are usually stimulating. The easy availability of a wide variety of interesting reading materials is indispensible. These materials, such as paperbacks, magazines, puzzle books, etc., must be available in the classrooms, not just stored formally in a library, and protected by a complicated check-out system. (See Chapter Twelve, "The Adolescent Slower Learner's Classroom: Contents and Appearance" for some comments on these materials.

But whether or not an adolescent slower learner becomes a reader is a problem of wider ramifications. A teacher can help a student break the un-reading cycle, and if the break is successful, as it often is, that student's life will be effectively changed. To encourage that student to enter the universe of books permanently however, the teacher must turn to the rest of the world for help.

CHAPTER NINE

A Cognitive Curriculum for Slower Learners: Creative, Logical and Critical Thinking

The nurturing of the cognitive skills of productive thinking should assume a central place in the curriculum, not a secondary or incidental one. Training of these skills should not be subordinated to the overriding demands of subject matter acquisition as at present, but should be dealt with directly. What we need, in short, is a "cognitive curriculum", one which nurtures the process of productive thinking in its own right . . . .
(Covington, 1967.)

It is a central purpose of education to train these cognitive skills of productive thinking, thus preparing the student for the effective and personally rewarding use of the mind with whatever subject matter and whatever problems he may have to deal.
(Crutchfield, 1969.)

Flying Blind With J-17

J-17 was a class of thirty-eight adolescent slower leaners whom I taught early in my career. Perhaps "taught" does not reflect with much accuracy, the actual sequence of events with J-17. Rather it was more a case of initial confrontation, then curiosity, a slow development of mutual near-trust, and finally, interest and enjoyment. I taught. But most of all, I learned.

J-17 and I did not come together in the normal fashion. They were not my class when the year began but we were neighbors, for they studied (?) English in the room next to mine, under a nervous, young woman just out of teacher's college.

They crucified her. In less than a month she was admitted to a psychiatric hospital and remained under intensive care for more than a year. The first replacement teacher left after one meeting with J-17. The second lasted two days. The administration didn't bother to hire a third; they *appointed* me.

Because I was new to the school, and relatively new to teaching, my colleagues offered a generous amount of unsolicited information about J-17. And what they left out, the students themselves supplied: "They just *cannot* read!" "They won't do anything!" "We're supposed to be kinda *dumb,* y'know." "We ain't gonna do *nuthin*'!" "Don't let Cathy excuse herself; she'll just spend an hour applying makeup." "She's a U.M." (unwed mother). "He's a probie." (on probation). "Keep them in their seats." "One piece of chalk in the room at a time." "Jim ain't gonna be here, he O.D.ed last night." (overdose of drugs).

109

J-17 was to be my first *real* challenge. In the years since, I have realized that they were typical adolescent slower learners in some ways, unique in others. Their uniqueness I think, was owing to the size of the group. Thirty-eight is a large number. Every negative act, every misdemeanor, every disinclination by a single student, was compounded by thirty-seven different reactions. As for being typical, there isn't a teacher of adolescent slower learners who has never heard: "I won't." "I can't." "This is dumb!" "It stinks!" "We done that already."

As J-17's English teacher, I faced a situation that over years of experience, has become all too familiar. Most of them could read, but wouldn't. There was no point in assigning homework; it would never be attempted. Literature, they felt, was for "queers". (A student in J-17 once asked me in all sincerity, if it was true that English teachers wore their clothes to bed!) In fact, with J-17, I could be certain of only one thing. These students could *think*. And if any proof of that was needed, one had only to reflect on some of the incredibly detailed and intricate schemes they devised to avoid work, or to explain an unauthorized absence, or to conceal some mischievous act. Not until I realized this — or to be more honest, *admitted* it — did I find the key to helping J-17 learn. From this realization grew a kind of "cognitive curriculum", a curriculum which has been successful — amazingly so — with slower learner classes ever since.

The principle behind it is simple. Although many adolescent slower learners are unwilling or unable to deal comfortably with symbolic, academic material, they are willing and able to indulge in the *thought processes themselves*. Exercises in the cognitive processes, if carefully designed for success, can help to develop the confidence and the ability these students need for living life to the full as they see it. Practice in creative, logical and critical thinking, each for its own sake, should then be an integral part of the slower learner's program.

J-17 At Work, Creatively, Logically and Critically
Here are a few random examples of J-17's work in this "cognitive curriculum". The work is essentially non-academic, but academic achievement is not its purpose.

> For about thirty seconds, examine this figure carefully. How many reasonable questions can you ask about it?

J-17 was given two minutes to respond to this task. In this period of time the class was able to generate 107 *different,* reasonable questions about that figure. The importance is not so much *what* questions they asked, but rather that a class of adolescent slower learners had developed the motivation and flexibility of mind to ask that many!*

Before reading on to J-17's responses to the problem below, consider what response you yourself might give.

> Mutt and Jeff are playing golf. The loser has to buy dinner, so the two watch each other very closely. At the fourth tee, Jeff makes a near-perfect shot to the green, almost a hole-in-one, but by some strange twist of fate, the ball rolls into a paper bag which has blown onto the green. Mutt will not allow the ball to be removed without a penalty; Jeff has to play the ball without touching it with his hands. Can you suggest a solution for Jeff which will not cost him a penalty stroke?

With one exception, every member of the class was able to generate a creative solution. The most popular solution was to burn the paper bag. Non-useful solutions, they rejected. (e.g., One member suggested a dynamite charge nearby which would cause the earth to heave and the ball to roll out of the bag!) Another solution: "Put the ball into the ball washer and then back into the bag while still wet. After waiting a few minutes, the wetness will have weakened the paper sufficiently to remove the bag without moving the ball." (This solution caused such fierce argument that an actual field test was conducted under the guidance of J-17's science teacher. Regrettably, it did not work).

J-17 attacked this problem in small groups using the brain-storming approach.

> Your eccentric uncle has died, and in his will has left you one ton of broken peanut shells per week, from his peanut butter cannery. How many ideas can you think of, for using this odd gift?

In three minutes, the average number of acceptable ideas per group — that is, acceptable to themselves — was approximately forty. Their ideas included the usual items one would anticipate from a brainstorming session on a problem like this: use the shells as packing; as fertilizer; as mulch; as food; paint them and make a mobile; use them in jumping pits for track and field events; etc. But each group was also able to generate some very original uses too: glue the shells to an attractive

---

* By the time they were given this problem, and those that follow, J-17 had already been given a fair bit of practice in this work.

piece of cloth and lay it at one's front door as a nighttime burglar-alarm-*mat;* use them as an ecologically safe means for providing traction for car tires spinning on ice during the winter; etc.

Simple — and complicated — puzzles in logic formed yet another part of J-17's curriculum. The puzzle that follows was solved by every member of the class, some of them of course taking a great deal longer than others, for it is fairly involved.

Listed below are some comments about the nine members of a baseball team. With a little study and reasoning, you should be able to figure out what position each holds on the team.

1. Joe and the third baseman lived in the same building.
2. Bob, Joe, Frank and the catcher were beaten at golf by the second baseman.
3. Ed was a very close friend of the catcher.
4. The centre fielder was taller than the right fielder.
5. The shortstop, the third baseman and Frank each liked to go to the races.
6. The pitcher's wife was the third baseman's sister.
7. Bill's sister was engaged to the second baseman.
8. Bob and Harry each won $5 from the pitcher at poker.
9. The catcher and the third baseman each had two children.
10. Jim decided to get a divorce.
11. All of the battery and infield, excepting Harry, Joe and Ed, were shorter than Jim.
12. Bill and the outfielders liked to play gin rummy together whenever they could.
13. Jack was taller than Frank. Tom was shorter than Frank. Each of them weighed more than the first baseman.
14. One of the outfielders was either Tom or Ed.
15. Bill, Bob and Jack, the centre fielder, and the right fielder were bachelors. The others were married.
16. Bob, Ed, and the shortstop were teetotallers.

The following chart, used by Ted, a fifteen-year-old boy in the class (and an avid baseball fan) demonstrates the kind of thinking and self-application these problems can encourage.*

---

* This solution, incidentally, was reached by Ted in my presence. It took him exactly 19 minutes. I have yet to see any adult equal that time.

	Cat.	Pit.	1st	2nd	3rd	S.S.	R.F.	C.F.	L.F.	Marr.	Bach.
Joe	X	▓	X	X	X	X	X	X	X	√	
Bob	X	X	▓	X	X	X	X	X	X		√
Frank	X	X	X	X	X	X	X	▓	X		
Ed	X	X	X	X	▓	X	X	X	X	√	
Jack	X	X	X	▓	X	X	X	X	X		√
Tom	X	X	X	X	X	X	▓	X	X		
Harry	▓	X	X	X	X	X	X	X	X	√	
Bill	X	X	X	X	X	▓	X	X	X		√
Jim	X	X	X	X	X	X	X	X	▓	√	
Married	√	√			√				√		
Bachelor				√			√	√			

C.F. taller than R.F.
Pit's wife is 3rd's sister (combine 6 and 7)
Cat. has 2 kids
3rd has 2 kids
Jim — divorce
Harry, Joe, and Ed shorter than Jim
Jack taller than Frank
Tom is shorter than Frank
Tom or Ed is C.F., R.F., or L.F.
Bill, Bob, Jack, C.F., R.F., bachelor

Critical thinking also formed a part of this "cognitive curriculum". Frequently, J-17 would apply critical analysis to the results of a creative brainstorming session. At other times they would react individually to an ethical problem, and then in groups, analyze these individual reactions. As much as possible, the critical thinking exercises were coordinated with their writing programs. Here is an example of one of the pieces that resulted. It was written by Sara, aged 16. Although her spelling is less than perfect, her critical analysis is rather interesting.

Three Kinds of Teenage Drug Users

There are three mane categorys of heads, this is not counting the one-timers. They're not heads. The first kind is the escapers, the dangerous ones. For them turning on is really turning off. This bunch runs from things they can't handel. If they can't get pot or horse or speed they'll drink booze. And this is the group that is growing bigger. There are a lot of kids running from something.

The second group is the explorers. These guys will try anything for excitement. If it isn't motorbikes or hot cars it's acid or smack. They say they're expanding their conshusness but reelly they're just looking for thrills. This group isn't so dangerous for they stick pretty much to themselves. It mite even be said that a drop of acid in one of these kids is safer for society than the same kid in a hopped-up car.

Rebels are the third kind. I have a hard time explaining this group because I think I'm in it. Reelly, I guess it's that we reject our parents and the things they stand for. We don't like technology and pollution, we just don't like their world I guess. Like my old man. He says drugs are bad, but every weekend he's stone drunk. I think I had my first pot just because he said not too. And that's what all the rebels are like. But I'm beginning to reelize now that if even if we don't like our parents world, drugs aren't much of a replacement.

In her presentation of drug usage, Sara, in her own language comes very close to the position taken by many modern social psychologists. Her vocabulary and syntax would hardly qualify her for the pages of a learned journal, but it is obvious that she can *think*. Just as it was obvious that the rest of J-17 could *think*. And their thinking ability improved throughout the year. They became more flexible, more imaginative, more *courageous* (i.e. more willing to attempt problems *and* to report results), more curious, and certainly more positive. This is not to imply that some miracle occurred; many of J-17's unendearing habits remained. But they were a changed group. On the day I first met them, their fourth English teacher in a month, the class spokesman had greeted me with: "We already got rid of three, y'know!" The speaker was Ted, whose baseball solution appears on page 113.

So What!

In the many workshops, seminars, and lectures during which I have met hundreds of people who teach the adolescent slower learner, no proposal meets with a more dubious reaction initially, than the "cognitive curriculum". The reaction is more wary than it is negative. But it is understandable. Traditionally, classrooms in the western world have served as places where the acquisition of *knowledge* ranks uppermost; the gathering of specific facts often outstrips thinking in importance — certainly thinking for its own sake, or thinking which is not immediately productive of an "answer" that can be tested or graded.* Such an approach to education naturally makes the cognitive curriculum somewhat suspect.

Generally, the doubts seem to coalesce around five basic issues.

1. "But problem-solving isn't English!"

To this statement I am always tempted to respond: "What else have you tried lately?" Facetiousness, however, is the vanguard of weakness. Yes, it isn't English, but our primary job must still be to teach *students first,* and our subject second.

The vast majority of English teachers in the western world have a specifically academic background — usually several years of study in the various fields of literature. And it is only natural that they should want to teach their "field", their area of primary interest. Fortunately, a significant number of adolescents are willing to accept that "field", some because they wish to, and some because they are playing the game of "school". The slower learner, however, is often a different matter. Not only does he refuse to play the game of "school", but he particularly rejects literature for it has no immediately apparent value.

To attack this problem, even the most professionally dedicated teachers still approach it on an academic plane. They turn to diluted versions of the classics, abridgements, simplified series of one kind or another. The result, inevitably, is frustration: for the student because "it's still the same old stuff" and for the teacher because he is presenting watered-down material.

It seems reasonable then that an answer may lie in shifting the emphasis, temporarily at least, to something less academic. There are all kinds of achievements in our world which have no direct relation to academic accomplishment. Nor is academic success necessarily predictive of success in life. Then too, the joy of academic pursuit is not commonly felt by all mankind. On the other hand, the ability to *think* creatively, logically and critically, is possessed in some degree by all humans. Slower learners have this ability. And if by adolescence they have clearly demonstrated their disinclination toward purely academic study, then

---

* Of the many interesting studies on this issue, few are more revealing than that by Cox and Unks, 1967. (See book list at end of chapter.) They took items from randomly selected tests in Southern California high schools and applied them to B. S. Bloom's *Taxonomy of Educational Objectives.* Approximately 98% of the items they found were in the category, Knowledge, and approximately 75% were in the sub-category, Knowledge of Specific Facts. There were *no* items in Bloom's top two categories, Synthesis and Evaluation.

surely to relieve the frustration and at the same time to do something of value, the cognitive curriculum is worth a try.

2. "I can understand logical and critical thinking, but *creative* thinking? For the *slower learner?* What purpose does it serve?"

Initial motivation for one thing. At worst, creative thinking is something at which the adolescent slower learner has not yet failed. At best, it provides a new kind of challenge, an excitement he is not accustomed to feeling. My experiences indicate that adolescent slower learners attack creative problem solving with enthusiasm. Because they do not follow their normal penchant for dismissing things out of hand, a carefully constructed program in problem solving leading from success to success, can be the key factor in getting the slower learner re-activated to learning.

Creative problem solving is also a valuable technique for improving the *attitude* of slower learners. A student who is encouraged to begin again, can usually be encouraged to maintain a flexible, positive attitude, not only toward creative problem solving but toward all his other work as well. Successful problem solving gives the slower learner *courage.* It eliminates the if-at-first-you-don't-succeed-quit syndrome that seems to operate in all his endeavors.

Finally it serves the purpose of developing ideational fluency. A flexible mind, capable of producing good ideas, is not the sole property of highly intelligent or educated people. Slower learners are often close-minded, inflexible and terribly narrow because everyone — including themselves — expects them to be that way. Creative thinking situations are a way out of that morass. A mind that learns to be flexible in problem solving situations will apply that flexibility to other areas both in education and in life.

In sum, creative thinking for slower learners is a way to get them going again, a way to encourage positive, flexible, thinking. Admittedly, for some slower learners, its initial appeal will lay in its novelty and in its apparent lack of connection with "examinable" subjects. Be that as it may, if these factors are what can motivate an unmotivated student, then it is only right to use them.

3. "Yes, but can they *do* it?"

In a series of irregular and informal experiments using a group of 29 university graduates (mostly with degrees in English) and a group of nineteen adolescent slower learners (aged 12-16), I found that the latter group consistently matched or bettered their more educated counterparts in creative problem and puzzle solving. As a dramatic example — one of many — the following puzzle was solved by eighteen of the nineteen slower learners, in one and a half minutes. In the same space of time, only 14 of the graduates reached a solution.

> A farmer had five pieces of chain, each with three links. He wanted these five pieces joined into one, and went to a blacksmith who charged 1 cent per cut, and 1 cent per weld. The farmer naturally expected to pay eight cents for the job, but when he was about to pay for this work, the blacksmith charged only 6 cents. What did the blacksmith do?

The slower learners' generally high rate of success, relative to the rate of the graduates is owing in part to the amount of practice they had in puzzle solving. But I believe that one more factor operates here. The graduates, because of years of thinking along specific, rather rigid lines, had lost or perhaps never developed the kind of flexibility that is needed to attack puzzle solving. They tended to think in a linear fashion. The slower learners, partly because of their age and partly because of their lack of academic training had not yet developed this kind of "tracked" thinking. (There is no doubt in my mind that given the same degree of exposure to puzzle solving, however, the graduates would probably have outstripped the slower learners in rate and speed of success.) The conclusion that one can draw from this, nevertheless, is that slower learners *are capable* of creative puzzle and problem solving.

4. "Is the whole curriculum made up of puzzles and social problems? Is there ever a short story, or a novel, or a play?"

Problem and puzzle solving are a vital part of the cognitive curriculum. They are particularly useful as initial motivators for a class that, like J-17, has made its negative position obvious. They form excellent points around which practice in oracy, writing and listening may polarize. But they are not intended to be the whole curriculum and they are not intended to *replace* literature.

The cognitive curriculum is as much an attitude as it is a "thing". It can form the basis of an approach to literature in which students, rather than memorize the characteristics of a short story, brainstorm solutions for the dilemma faced by the hero of a short story. Instead of concerning themselves with expressionism and impressionism in Arthur Miller's *Death of A Salesman,* students would concern themselves with the problems of production, or seek out alternatives for Willy

Loman, or relate their own values critically to Willy's. The cognitive curriculum does not scan poetry or analyze rhyme schemes, or point out the differences between blank verse and free verse. Rather, it seeks out and tries to imagine what the poet felt. It encourages the student to write poetry himself. A cognitive curriculum is one that emphasizes *thinking* for its own sake and anything that will serve that end — puzzles, problems, literature, newspapers, magazines — becomes a part of it.

5. And what does research evidence say?

It would be easy to cite some of the many articles and studies which point out the lack of curriculum aimed at developing creativity and productive thinking. One comment however, is worth noting. It appears as a footnote in the famous Bloom *Taxonomy of Educational Objectives* (Cognitive Domain).*

> Recent writing and research on creativeness and productive think- ing (which overlap with synthetic abilities) attest to the importance attached to these problems by many psychologists and educators. The recent challenge by Allison Davis and others is worth noting at this point. Allison Davis and Robert D. Hess, "What About IQs?" *Journal of the National Education Association 38* (Nov., 1949), pp. 604-605. Kenneth Eells and others, *Intelligence and Cultural Differences* (Chicago: University of Chicago Press, 1951, xii, p. 388.) After demonstrating that conventional intelligence tests underrate the ability of children from lower socio-economic levels, they conclude that we are depriving ourselves of untapped re- sources of human ability and robbing such children of their right of full development. Furthermore, because most pupils get limited experience in genuine problem solving, these investigators believe that present programs retard pupils of low occupational groups by two years, on the average, after they have been in school only four years! Certainly this indictment demands serious attention.

Interestingly, the two pieces to which Bloom refers, were published in 1949 and 1951. It is apparent that little has been done in the inter- vening quarter century.

I
Creative Thinking At Work in the Classroom

What follows is a suggested outline only, for every teacher plans accord- ing to the nature and needs of each class. My own experience (chiefly

---

* B. S. Bloom et al., *Taxonomy of Educational Objectives* (New York: David McKay, 1956.)

learning from mistakes) suggests, however, that the program should be governed by a few specific principles.

1. Simple puzzles, requiring a minimum of reading, and usually involving some visual diagram or objects to be manipulated, make the best beginning. (Because they are highly motivating, the puzzles are valuable in breaking the un-reading cycle. But always begin with puzzles requiring minimal reading effort.)

2. At first, allow each student to work individually, and to progress in creative problem solving at his own rate.

3. Constantly encourage the students to suspend their *judgment* in the initial phases of creative problem solving. Otherwise, the critical faculty will inevitably jam the creative faculty.

4. Especially at the beginning of the program, do not hesitate to give as much assistance as possible — even to the point of "giving away" solutions.

5. Group problem solving is more successful if launched *after* the students have considerable experience working individually.

6. Creative problem solving, particularly the use of puzzles, should not occupy the whole of the students' time. Although there should be some concentration of time in this area at first, every effort should be made to continue the class programs in verbal fluency, writing, reading, concurrently with the creative thinking program.

7. Whatever the source of your puzzles, it is often helpful to rewrite the problems, using terminology and situations familiar to the students.

8. For brainstorming sessions on wider issues, the classic book in the field is Alex Osborne's *Applied Imagination* (New York: Charles Scribner's Sons, 1953). Osborne is the founder of the Creative Education Foundation.* Further excellent material comes from Dr. Sidney Parnes' *Instructor's Manual and Student Workbook,* available from the Foundation.

9. Although the program will gradually grow away from puzzle solving toward larger issues, it is helpful to return to it intermittently.

---

* Buffalo State University College, Chase Hall, 1300 Elmwood Avenue, Buffalo, New York, U.S.A. 14222.

Suggested Outline

(The amount of time and effort spent on each step should be altered according to students' needs. Examples are provided here, for purposes of explanation, but for a useful program, many more exercises should be added at each step.)

Step One: Beginning as *visually* and as *simply* as possible, introduce several puzzles of a nature and difficulty similar to these.

1. Retrace this drawing without retracing a line, and without lifting your pen from the paper.

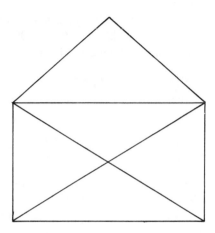

2. Repeat 1 without crossing a line.

3. Retrace this figure, without crossing a line, without retracing a line, without taking your pen off the paper.

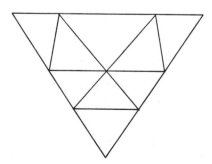

4. Under the same conditions as 3, retrace this figure.

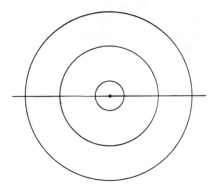

Note that these puzzles are basically all the same type. Although the shapes differ, the principle of solution does not change. Throughout this step, students should be encouraged to keep trying, and to try different attacks if their first few do not work. Above all, encourage them to be as free-wheeling and as flexible as they can be.

This step may take up several consecutive periods of class time. It is usually a good idea to go directly to Step Two without introducing anything else (writing, literature) in the interim.

Step Two: Introduce puzzles that have more reading connected to them. Although they may be as simple as those in Step One, they will appear to be more difficult. The visual aspects may be reduced somewhat in this step.

1. Mr. Jones got off the train in Halifax and in the station met a friend he hadn't seen in years. With his friend was a little girl.
"Glad to see you" said Jones.
"Same here!" replied the friend. "Did you know that I've gotten married? This is my little girl."
"How are you?" said Jones to the girl. "What's your name?"
The little girl replied, "Same as my mother."
"Then you must be Anne," said Jones. How did he know?

2. Two fathers and two sons went hunting. Each shot a duck and none shot the same duck — yet only 3 ducks were shot. How could this be?

3. A train leaves Montreal at 25 m.p.h. headed for Boston. At the same time, a train leaves Boston at 50 m.p.h. headed for Montreal. When they meet, which one will be nearer to Montreal?

4. The knights who live in the five castles below are bitter enemies. No one will cross the path of another for it will cause a fight to the death. One day, all five arrive at their stables together, and must get to their castles quickly because there is soon to be a downpour which will rust their armour. Can you design routes for them so that no one will cross another's path?

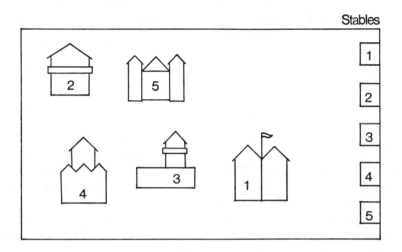

Stables

Unlike the problems in Step One, these in Step Two are less given to trial and error. Rather, the problems in Step Two are more given to the "flash-of-insight" typical of creative thinking.* The knights' problem in 4 for example, is a simple one, once one realizes that the solution lies in going behind some of the castles. Flexibility in 2 is vital. In 3, a solution is immediately apparent once one realizes that the rates of speed are meaningless.

---

* The "Flash-of-insight" is an integral part of the creative thinking process. It is a popular belief that this kind of illumination occurs in an *instant,* such as on the day in 1685 when Isaac Newton saw an apple fall in his garden at Woolsthorpe. And the popular belief is often accurate. Darwin, in his autobiography wrote: "I can remember the very spot in the road, whilst in my carriage, when to my joy the solution occurred to me."

But what is often ignored is the flexibility in the mind which achieves these flashes of insight. For example the following little puzzle often stymies even the most apparently free-thinking adults.

Add to this sequence:

O,T,T,F,F, ...

Most people approach this puzzle by attempting to find a clue in the relative position these letters have in the alphabet. But a tenacious flexible thinker, however, tries to see how many *different* ways the sequence has meaning. (One, Two, Three, Four, Five, ...)

Problem 1 introduces another important phase of creative problem solving: verification. Although it is vital to suspend judgment when one is attacking a problem, it is equally vital to verify, once a solution has been reached. Many students respond to 1 with "Well, they were friends, so the man getting off the train would naturally know whom his friend married". That answer, of course, breaks down in verification.

Consequently, it is useful in Step Two to give several problems which teach the need for verification. Like the "friends at the train station" problem, these must be problems which require a flash of creative insight, but which then require a few more stages of verifiable thinking. A few simple examples follow:

5. A toad starts to climb out of an abandoned well. The well is 16 feet deep. Each day he climbs four feet, and each night he slips back 3 feet. How long does it take him to get out?

6. You have a 3 gallon measure and a 5 gallon measure, and what you *need* is exactly 4 gallons of water. How would you do it?

7. A farmer was asked how many ducks he had and he replied: "Well, they just went down the path a minute ago, and I saw one duck ahead of two ducks, a duck behind two ducks, and a duck between two ducks. How many ducks did he have?

Step Three: This step is merely a follow up of Steps One and Two, but now, problems are introduced which require more concentration and tenacity, perhaps a greater depth of insight, more reading and more involved verification.

Students might be encouraged to present more detailed, written responses. Or they might be put in groups to discuss solutions — whatever means the teacher feels will be most useful for their own development.

Examples:

1. A bee was sitting on an automobile travelling 30 miles an hour. Some distance away, another automobile was approaching, also at 30 miles an hour. When the two cars were exactly 30 miles apart, the bee left the first car and flew to the second at the incredible speed of 70 miles per hour. Then he turned round and sped back to the first. He kept this up until the two cars met. How many miles did the bee travel?

2. To prevent bickering after his death, an old king divided his land among his four sons with perfect fairness. Each son had a plot equal in size and identical in shape to the plots his brother inherited. Since the land is odd-shaped, how did the king accomplish this?

The Land

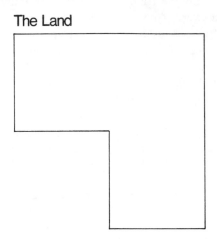

During Step Three, or perhaps *after* it is completed, or maybe during Step Two — whenever the teacher deems it appropriate — it is often effective to introduce a short story for the purpose of fostering creativity. The story should be one primarily of *plot,* the more complicated the action, the better. Teacher and students read the story together but they stop at the main crisis, the point at which the hero faces a dilemma. Here, each student should be encouraged to present as many solutions for the hero as possible before going on with the story.

By Step Three, the amount of time spent specifically on this cognitive program should decrease somewhat in favor of the other programs — writing, reading, oral fluency, listening. That is, simply under the age-old teaching principle of variety, students should be following a number of development programs simultaneously.

Step Four: By this time, students are usually ready for yet another stage in the development of their creative thinking ability: practice in the *production* of ideas.

Students are given problems to work on in groups, utilizing the technique of brainstorming (as described and popularized by A. F. Osborne in *Applied Imagination*). For slower learners this is a particularly important stage for it encourages production of ideas in quantity, and provides practice as well, in listening and verbalizing.

Two basic principles are of overwhelming importance here. Since the purpose of such a technique as brainstorming is to develop a flexible mind, there must be *total deferment of judgment*. No idea is a bad one; all ideas, no matter how ridiculous they may seem at first, must be acceptable. The second principle is that *quantity* of ideas at this stage is more important than quality.*

1. Provide a few warm-up exercises simply to loosen the students' "idea-tanks".

    (a) Bring a tin can to class, or a brick, or a rubber ball, a coat hanger, or a stick. *The Problem:* In three minutes, think of how many uses you can find for each. Try for fifty.

    (b) What would we have to do without today, if the wheel had never been discovered?

    (c) How many as yet uninvented electrical appliances can you think of for your home?

Initially, slower learners' responses are often quite slow in coming, and quite low in quantity. But after several brainstorming sessions over several days, their ideational fluency will improve to the point where a group of slower learners will easily outdistance — in quantity of ideas — a group of well-educated, but unpracticed adults.

2. Introduce more complicated problems such as those that follow. It is important to remember that no one solution is necessarily the right one; there may be several. The important thing is to produce ideas with total suspension of judgment. Then, when the number of ideas is large enough, submit them to as careful a verification as possible under the circumstances. The problems outlined below *actually did occur,* and were solved, but the solutions that slower learners may devise could be equally as good as those that were ultimately used.

    (a) A trainee pilot has taken off from an airport on his first solo flight. By nightfall he has become hopelessly lost. He has no

---

* I attended my first brainstorming session in 1954. One of the problems we were given was: "How would you improve television sets?" At that time, in Canada anyway, television was in a relatively primitive state. Those few homes with television had little table model sets with tiny screens and limited reception. As a consequence, these ideas from a group with no technical knowledge at all were quite "far out" — in 1954: 1. Enlarge the screen to at least 2 feet square. 2. Put the set in a cabinet; make it a piece of furniture. 3. Develop a remote control so that the set can be adjusted from one's chair. 4. Eliminate aerials. 5. Introduce color. 6. Put the tubes all in one drawer for easy access at repair time. 7. Record programs electronically so that they can be plugged into a set at the viewer's discretion. There were many other ideas which, like those above, are a reality today. (KJW)

night flying equipment. He radios the airport and explains his predicament.

If you were the air traffic controller, how would you help him?

(b) A hollow cylinder float controls a valve which prevents a reservoir from overflowing. The float is about the size of a pail, and is made of finely tooled galvanized metal. It is discovered that this cylinder has sprung a leak, so small that it is invisible to the naked eye, but water is definitely seeping in. You have no microscope. And there is no replacement part available. You must find the leak and repair it, or the float will fill with water, sink, and open the valve, causing the reservoir to overflow.

How would you do it?

(c) Before the coming of the white man, seals were vital to the survival of the Eskimo. Traditionally the Eskimos harpooned seals at breathing holes in the ice. They faced a problem though. Seals usually stick just their nose out of the water, so the hunter had to be right *at* the hole. Also, seals have acute hearing under water, and when they hear footsteps near a breathing hole, they may avoid that hole indefinitely.

Can you suggest how the Eskimos dealt with the problem of getting to a hole without being discovered?

Step Five: There is no final stage to a program in creative thinking. Step Five is more of a level toward which slower learners should work. (And they attain it with an ease that would surprise most adults.) At this level, three kinds of activity seem to be most useful. First, there is still the intermittent use of puzzles; secondly, brainstorming sessions on such problems as those in Step Four — again on an intermittent basis*; and thirdly, a creative thinking style of approach to reading exercises, short stories, novels, drama, etc.

If they have reached this level most slower learners will gradually drop "No I can't! (or won't)" in favor of "In how many ways can I....". This kind of attitude has a profound effect on all areas of their schooling. Specifically, they develop a considerably more positive attitude toward those things with which English teachers are more familiar and comfortable.

For example, the approach to the short story outlined earlier in this chapter, in which students brainstorm options for the hero in his

---

* An effective variation at this stage is to have students themselves think of and propose problems for group sessions. Also, working individually, have them privately brainstorm a real, personal problem.

dilemma, leads to some interesting aspects of literary study. After the students have produced a quantity of ideas which the hero of a short story might be expected to follow to solve his dilemma, *verification* can be attempted under these guidelines:

> What solution offered would be most consistent with the hero's *character*?
>
> Which solution would be most affected by the *setting* of the story?
>
> Has the writer/narrator prepared readers for a specific kind of solution?

A similar approach is effective in other genres as well. To a class that reads only with great reluctance, the daily newspaper offers a variety of short, immediate situations to which creative thinking can be applied. Short films offer the same opportunity, as does commercial television. The possibilities for thinkers with flexibility and a positive attitude are unlimited.

II
Logical Thinking At Work In The Classroom*

Of the many benefits that slower learning adolescents gain from practice in logical thinking for its own sake, there are certain ones which seem to be outstanding in importance.

As with creative thinking, the motivational factor encourages *reading* by students who normally read only with great reluctance.

To solve any problem logically, one needs a certain degree of *tenacity,* particularly if trial and error is the method being used. For slower learners, tenacity is a particularly important virtue to develop since it is a significant factor in overcoming one of their worst shortcomings: fear.

Organization likewise plays an integral part, for many of the problems in this unit require the handling and retention of multiple pieces of information.

In my own experience I have found that slower learning adolescents, while they are quite able to comprehend what is required in a logical problem, sometimes fail to achieve a solution because of a flaw

---

* This program in logical thinking for slower learners is not the course that many teachers have encountered in university (compete with syllogisms, and like terminology). There is nothing to prevent a teacher using that approach however, if in his opinion it will be useful.

in *execution*. This same feature of course, is true of much of their studies. Thus practice in logical problem solving for its own sake can have a profound effect — as with creative thinking — on all other aspects of the slower learners' education. Practice in solving small puzzles and problems in logic can teach them to approach other things with care, with caution, and with courage.

A difficulty arises here, in the question of whether or not the pedagogy of this program in logical thinking conflicts with creative thinking, since on the surface they require behaviors which are diametrically opposed. In fact, however, creative thinking and logical thinking are complementary. Life itself presents situations which demand in some cases the deferred-judgment, free-wheeling thinking of creativity, and in other cases the cautious approach of logic, and in some cases, both styles. Solutions often lie in the choice of which style to employ, and when. Practice in this kind of decision-making then for slower learners, has both short and long range value.

Step One: Like the program in creative thinking, practice in logic begins best with simple puzzle situations, the simpler the better at first, for success will build courage.

1. Continue these sequences.
   1, 2, 4, 7, 11, —————
   4, 5, 7, 11, 19, —————
   6, 3, 9, 6, —————

2. If it takes one minute per cut, how long will it take to cut a 12 foot pole into one-foot pieces?

Step Two: Increase gradually, the complexity of the problems, and demonstrate to the students how asking questions can help solve problems. For example, this age-old problem:

A man owned a fox, a duck, and a bag of corn. One day he was on the bank of a river, where there was a boat large enough for him to cross with only one of his possessions. If he left the fox and duck alone, the fox would eat the duck. If he left the duck and the corn alone, the duck would eat the corn. The river was too rough for the duck to swim. How did he get safely across the river with all three of his possessions?

Can he take the fox first? (Duck will eat corn) If he takes the corn first? (Fox will eat duck) Therefore he takes the duck first. Then he takes either the fox or the corn. But on the other side he will be faced with a similar problem. Let us assume he takes the fox. This would leave the fox and the duck on the other side while he fetches the corn. What to do? If he brings the fox back, he will be no farther ahead: therefore, bring the duck back, leave it and take the corn over where it will be safe with the fox. Then he comes back to get the duck.

After such a problem, it is usually wise to follow with one that requires the same kind of logical approach.

> Three soldiers and three prisoners must cross a river too rough to swim. There is a boat which will hold only two people at one time. The prisoners have sworn an oath not to escape but the soldiers feel it would be unwise to be outnumbered on either side of the river. How can they get across without the soldiers ever being outnumbered on either side?

Step Three: Introduce problems which give practice in handling multiple pieces of information. Again the complexity of these should increase gradually. Demonstate to students the value of making charts, diagrams, etc., when dealing with multiple pieces of information.

For example:

> You have three playing cards in a row, on a table. There is at least one five just to the right of a four. There is at least one five just to the left of a five. There is at least one spade just to the left of a heart, and there is at least one spade just to the right of a spade. What are the three cards.

The solution demands a chart. Draw the three cards side by side.

Then deal with known information. There is at least one *five* just to the *right* of a *four*.

4   5

There is at least one *five* just to the *left* of a *five*.

4   5   5

We now know that the cards are:

The same kind of thinking will show the cards to be spade, spade, heart.

Hence the cards are:

4 spades	5 spades	5 hearts

The more complex problem below can also be solved with the use of a similar chart to regulate the known information.

Three men, Jack, Reg, and Winston are of different ages. Jack is a bachelor. Reg earns less money than the youngest of the three. The oldest of the three earns most, but he has his son enrolled in an expensive military school for which he pays high fees. Who is the eldest, and who is the youngest man?

Known information.

Names	married?	money?	age?
Jack	bachelor		cannot be eldest
Reg		earns least	cannot be youngest
Winston			

The entire solution can be accomplished on the chart, but for purposes of this example, the chart includes only the minimum information one can write down before needing to apply logic. Since the eldest, who earns most, has a son, the eldest cannot be Jack. We know it is not Reg, because of the earning factor. Therefore the eldest is Winston. Since Reg cannot be the youngest, that one must be Jack.

One of the goals of Step Three, of course, is to lead ultimately to the complexity of such problems as *Who's Who on the Baseball Team?* presented along with Ted's solution, earlier in this chapter.

Step Four: Although it is helpful to return to puzzles on an intermittent basis, one of the objectives of practice in logical thinking is to have slower learners apply logical perception to longer pieces of prose. The usefulness of such an exercise in a reading program is self-evident. Its usefulness as training in the development of cognitive processes should be equally obvious. The exercise that follows is an example of the type of classroom activity one can use. It was voted by J-17 as the most interesting logic problem of the year.

"The Bertha Huse Case"
from William James: On Psychical Research

The following incident took place in New Hampshire, in 1898. It is recorded in *Proceedings, The American Society For Psychical Research,* Volume I, Part II, 1907. The main account of the incident is written by Dr. Harris Kennedy, a medical doctor, and at the time, an assistant instructor at Harvard Medical school. Several corroborative statements follow this account, written either by witnesses or by people intimately involved. *Yes, They Can!* in an effort to save space, prints only one of these statements, since they are essentially identical to the statement made by Sullivan.

Dr. Kennedy's Account

On Monday, Oct. 31st, 1898, Miss Bertha Huse left her home at Enfield, N.H., at 6 a.m., before the rest of the family had risen. She took her way down the street toward the so-called Shaker Bridge. On her way she was seen by several people, and by one person when she was on the bridge. Her family, learning of her absence, instituted a search for her, and during the greater part of the day 150 men, more or less, hunted the woods and lake shore in that vicinity. This search proving of no avail, Mr. Whitney, a mill owner of Enfield, sent to Boston for divers, with a suitable outfit. A diver named Sullivan worked the better part of all Tuesday, and up to Wednesday noon, without success in the lake.

On Wednesday evening, Nov. 2nd, Mrs. Titus, of Lebanon, N.H., a village about four and one-half miles from Enfield, while dozing after supper, aroused the attention of her husband, who was seated near her, by her noises, and extremely horrified countenance. When he spoke to her, she failed to answer, and it was necessary for him to shake her before arousing her to consciousness. When she was conscious, the first thing she said was, "Why did you disturb me? In a moment I should have found that body." After this she told her husband, "If I behave very peculiarly tonight, or cry out, or seem greatly disturbed, do not on any account awaken me, but leave me to myself." At some time during the night Mr. Titus was aroused by the screams of his wife. He got up, lit a lamp, and waited, obeying his wife's instructions. She, during a following interval, though not awake, spoke in substance as follows:

"She followed the road down to the bridge, and on getting part way across it, stepped out onto that jutting beam which was covered with white frost. There she stood undecided whether to go into the water there or go up over the hill to the pond. While so standing, she slipped on the log, fell backwards, and slid in underneath the timber work of the bridge. You will find her lying, head in, and you will only be able to see one of her rubbers projecting from the timber work."

Early in the morning, at her earnest solicitation, her husband went to Mr. Ayer, an employee of the Mascoma Flannel Co., at Lebanon, and asked him for leave to absent himself from the mill that morning, in order to go with his wife to the Shaker Bridge at Enfield. He then told Mr. Ayer the story, substantially as above. Mr. Titus also told the story to Mr. W. R. Sunderlin, as well as to certain other persons, all in Lebanon, before he went with his wife to Enfield, where he told other parties of this occurrence, and asked Mr. Whitney, who had been foremost in the search, to accompany him and his wife to the spot his wife was desirous of investigating. When they reached the bridge, Mrs. Titus pointed out a certain spot where she said they would find the body in the position as above mentioned. Mr. Whitney, who was then one of quite a number at the spot, sent a messenger to get the diver who had been working in the neighbourhood of that spot on the previous days. On his arrival Mrs. Titus pointed out to him the spot where she said the body lay. He said, "I searched there yesterday, and found nothing." She said, "Yes, you searched *there*, and *there* (pointing to certain spots), but you did not search *there*, and if you go down, you will find only the rubber of her shoe projecting from the timber work." To satisfy her, he put on his diving suit, and went down at the spot indicated. After a moment or two, the bonnet of the deceased rose to the surface, and shortly after the diver came up bringing the body. The diver then said, "I did not look in this place yesterday, as the brush and debris were so thick there that I could not see; in fact, all I could feel of the body, was the rubber, projecting from the timber work."

Mrs. Titus's grandmother is said to have had a similar power in her day, but Mrs. Titus is not known to have made any pretense of being a clairvoyant, having never used her trances for any pecuniary reward, or for the sake of any notoriety. On the day following, viz., Nov. 4th, Mrs. Titus was ill.

Corroborative Statements

Here follow the statements of several of the persons named in the preceding story. They were written down by Dr. Kennedy from their lips a few days after the occurrences, read by him to them, and signed by them as accurate.

Corroborative statements were written by Mr. Ayers, Mr. Sunderlin, Mr. Titus, Mr. Whitney, and the diver, Mr. Sullivan.

Sullivan's Statement

Nov. 21st, 1898, Mr. Sullivan, the diver in the Enfield case, was seen, at Simpson's dry dock, in East Boston. Being questioned in regard to the finding of Miss Huse, he told the following story:

"I was employed by the Boston Towboat Co., to search the Mascoma Lake. I went up at 7:10 Monday from Boston, arrived at night, and spent the greater part of Tuesday and Wednesday,

Nov. 2nd, from 10 a.m. until 3:10 p.m. in searching along the Shaker Bridge, We had given up the idea of diving, and I telephoned to Boston for powder, intending to go down by the early morning train and have the powder meet me at Union Station, and take the next train up, having about 20 minutes in Boston, and return with the powder. In the morning, before I could leave Enfield, Mr. and Mrs. Titus drove over from Lebanon and called on Mr. Whitney. Mr. Titus told Mr. Whitney the story of his wife's trance, and said that although he did not take much stock in it himself, he felt that on her account he ought to tell Mr. Whitney about it, simply to satisfy his wife. Mr. Whitney laughed, and said that he did not take any stock in it, and at the same time sent for me. We all went to the bridge, and Whitney told me that *although* he did not have much faith in it himself, he felt that there might be people in the village who did, and as long as we had started to do all we could to recover the body, we ought at least to give this woman a chance. I said that the villagers up there thought that the missing girl had taken to the woods, and therefore they had had searching parties, while I was dragging the lake; but I told him that I was there, waiting his orders, my business was to find the body, and I was willing to do anything that he said, adding at the same time, that I did not want to be made a fool of by going down in a variety of places that she might point out along the bridge. He said, "No," that she simply would pick out one place, and he thought the least we could do was to go down at the place she picked out, and that would satisfy the villagers.

Mrs. Titus walked along the bridge, and came to a spot and said, "This looks like the spot I saw in my trance," then after a moment's hesitation she said, "No, not exactly," and walked a little way along and stopped at another point, and said, "This looks very much more like the place that I saw last night." She stood there looking over the rail of the bridge from 20 minutes to half an hour. At last she said she was sure that was the place. I asked Mr. Whitney what I should do, and he said I had my suit, and he thought I had better go down in that spot. I took a guide line with sinker, located the spot from the bridge, threw the sinker over some little way from the bridge, as near as possible to the spot she pointed out. I then placed the ladder, and put on my suit, and went down. Mrs. Titus had told me the body was lying head down, only one foot with a new rubber showing, and lying in a deep hole. I started down the ladder, which extended about five feet under the water. When I swung off the ladder I went sideways and then turned. As I struck the crib work, 10 feet below the ladder, I turned to face the ladder, and my hand struck something. I felt of it, and it felt like a foot. I stopped short where I was: it is my business to recover bodies in the water, and I am not afraid of them, but in this instance I was afraid of the woman on the bridge. I thought to myself, "How can any woman come from four miles away and tell me or any other man where I would find this body?" I investigated and felt of her foot, and made sure that it was a body.

She was lying in a deep hole head down. It was so dark that I could not see anything. I had to feel entirely. I pulled her out, carried her up till I could get the light from above, and then arranged her clothing by laying her out on the crib of the bridge. When I had her laid out on the crib, I reached out for my guide line, but found I could not pull it up. I had to take out my knife and cut it as far as I could reach, and then I tied the line under her arms. The line was simply a clothes line (6 thread).

I then came up and asked for Mr. Whitney. I said, "She is down there." Mr. Whitney said, "I know it." I thought Mr. Whitney had been convinced pretty strongly. He said it turned out that when I pulled her out of the hole, her hat came off and rose to the surface, and Martin, who worked the pump for me, came near getting into trouble by being pushed off the bridge when the hat appeared on the surface, because the people rushed for the side of the bridge. Fortunately he was not pushed off.

We had a man there in a little skiff, who pulled her up. Mr. Whitney asked me what I thought of it, and I told him I did not think, I was *stunned*.

There are two statements which Mrs. Titus made that are absolutely correct. She located the place where I was to go down; also told me that the body was lying, head in, in a deep hole, with one foot sticking up, with a new rubber. I was down in about 18 feet of water. It was so dark, nobody could see anything down there. She must have seen the body as it was lying, because she described the position, and she had already pointed out the place I was to go down, and nobody could have known who had not seen the body as it was lying on the bottom. If you ask me how she knew it, I don't know; but if you ask me if I believe in it, why, I have been convinced against my will. If my best friend had told me, I should have thought he had seen a ghost. But if I ever have a similar case and can't find the body, I shall introduce the parties to Mrs. Titus, and she will find it.

[Signed] Michael J. Sullivan

Witnesses

Alfred Schaper,	Allen H. Cleghorn,
E. W. Taylor,	Harris Kennedy,
Geo. Burgess Magrath,	Langdon Frothingham,
E. A. Woods,	Alfred W. Balch,
Maynard Ladd,	Henry E. Hewes,
M. A. Potter,	William James.

The following questions served as guidelines for J-17.

1. There have been three significant attempts to explain the Bertha Huse Case scientifically, but each explanation seems inadequate. Can you point out *why* in each case?

(a) *The footprint theory*
If Bertha Huse was seen by several people before her disappearance, that means people were up and about at 6 a.m. If there was white frost on the beam from which she fell, it is quite likely that someone saw the footprints and was able to surmise where she had fallen, and how she lay in the water.

(b) *The witness theory*
Mrs. Titus may have actually witnessed the accident or may have been in league with the person who saw Bertha Huse on the bridge that morning. Seeking to gain fame, Mrs. Titus merely pretended clairvoyance.

(c) *The suicide theory*
Bertha Huse may have planned to commit suicide and may have conveyed her intention and probable method to Mrs. Titus.

2. In spite of the fact that all three theories are weak and probably wrong, there are still some doubts about the truth of Mrs. Titus' psychic powers. For example, why didn't *she* make a statement? Can you find any more flaws in the account?

Various accounts of psychic phenomena, extra-terrestrial activity, even some of Mao-Tse-Tung's writings have provided fertile material for my slower learner classes, as exercises in logic. I have also used material such as Sir Arthur Conan Doyles' novels (we amassed evidence as we read, attempting to solve the mysteries logically). And a first-rate source of exercises can be developed simply by tape-recording political speeches.

The amount of available material in which ill-logic predominates is unfortunately large. An objective of the cognitive curriculum is not only to help slower learners to see through that mass of ill-logic, but also, hopefully, to keep them from adding to it.

III
Critical Thinking At Work In The Classroom

Age-Old Scenario #329

Slower Learner 1: "You see the new kid yet?"
Slower Learner 2: "Yea, the one with fancy shoes?"
Slower Learner 1: "That's the one. He a Yougarian* y'know."
Slower Learner 2: "No kidding!"

---

* Read: Italian, Hungarian, Black, Indian, Oriental, Chicano, WASP, etc.

Slower Learner 1: "Watch him. They're tough!"
Slower Learner 2: "Who!"
Slower Learner 1: "Yougarians."
Slower Learner 2: "Ah. C'mon."
Slower Learner 1: "It's true! All Yougarians are *fighters!* I know. I see it on television!"

The damning proof. No further statement need be made. "I seen it on television. It's true!" "I know, 'cause I read it in the paper." "It's for sure, 'cause Sam told me!" Western society's tendency toward total, uncritical acceptance is magnified in the adolescent slower learner. There are few teachers who have never been stopped cold by the impenetrable wall of the slower learner's preconceptions.

The purpose of a program in critical thinking is to put a crack in that wall. Not that these students should become cynics, for in their own way they already display that characteristic. Rather, a program in critical thinking for its own sake, is designed essentially to foster the kind of broad-mindedness that theoretically grows out of what has been called a classical or literary education. Since so many slower learners simply do not stay in school long enough to attain that kind of broad-mindedness, and since so many of them in any case refuse to accept the content-material used in that classical style of education, an outflanking approach is at least worth investigating.

Most adolescent slower learners — even those like J-17 — can be brought to see the merits of critical questioning, the dangers of immediate total acceptance. They can learn to read the dangers of inflammatory rhetoric, the allurements in contemporary advertising methods. Above all, they can learn to recognize the impact of their own values on their life-outlook.

The practical stages in the critical thinking section of the cognitive curriculum need not be followed in the order shown below, since each stage is designed to develop a different aspect of the critical process.

Step One: The idea of this exercise is to present a situation, or give a statement from which an inference is drawn. The student then points out how a *different* inference may be taken from the situation or statement.

Statement: The Americans landed on the moon before the Russians.
Conclusion: The United States therefore must have superior scientists, technicans, and equipment.

For Discussion: For what other reasons may the United States have been first? More money? Better organization? Tighter scheduling? Coincidence?

The classroom methods for this exercise can vary widely. Students might work individually, in pairs, or in groups. A class may comb the daily newspaper either for *statements* or *conclusions* as above. Once each student has found an example, he or the whole class can develop alternative possibilities. Another situation is possible in which one student makes a *statement,* and submits it to a large group. Each member of the group draws a conclusion. The conclusions are compared and analyzed critically.

Editorials, gossip columns, polemical handbills, door-to-door advertising all provide relevant sources.

A few more examples follow; usually the best come from students.

1. *Statement:* Jackie Gleason is a successful entertainer.
   Conclusion: People feel that he drinks a lot, and he is successful because people like happy drinkers.

2. *Statement:* Women, on average, live three years longer than men.
   Conclusion: This is because they don't work as hard.

3. *Statement:* At intersections, the orange light is on for five seconds. Then the red light goes on. But before the light facing the opposite direction turns green, there is a three second delay.
   Conclusion: This is done so that cars approaching the intersection will have time to stop.

4. *Statement:* In the legends of Mesopotamia and in Greek mythology, there are stories of babies being abandoned by poor parents. These babies were discovered and raised by people of royal blood. This is what happened to Moses in the Old Testament.
   Conclusion: The story of Moses was simply copied from other stories.

5. *Statement:* When he was seventeen years old, Joey Brack who had never dated a girl in his life enrolled in a muscle-building program. Since then he has developed a reputation as a lady-killer.
   Conclusion: Girls fall for fellows with big muscles.

6. *Statement:* Frank Royal owns a shoe factory in Winnipeg. Every year between August and December he notices that larger and larger orders are sent in for rubber boots.
   Conclusion: Most people in Winnipeg buy rubber boots in the fall.

7. *Statement:* In North America, most people marry after the age of 20. In many Asian countries, people marry in their teens.
   Conclusion: Many Asians mature earlier than North Americans.

8. *Statement:* The suicide rate in apartment buildings is higher than in other types of dwellings.
   Conclusion: Apartment buildings are depressing and can lead people to suicide.

Step Two: To what degree is an individual influenced by his own values? How much of his critical awareness is based purely on "gut" reaction?

1. Present a basic situation.*

> Freddy K. has just driven out of the used car lot with his pur-
> chase, a four door hardtop, over-priced, but with all the options.
> Freddy barely had the money for a down payment, and the
> monthly payments will take 40% of his salary. When he signed the
> sales agreement Freddy paid no attention to the amount of actual
> interest, nor did he notice that if the car is repossessed he might
> still owe money that could be garnisheed from his wages. Freddy is
> married with three children. He has held his new job for only six
> months. His wife wishes he would spend his money on the family,
> but realizes that Freddy is very happy when he is driving a flashy
> car.

2. After students read the basic situation above, they individually record in a few sentences their reaction to what has happened. Then in groups, they discuss the situation using something like the following guidelines.

> (a) Should Freddy be allowed to buy a car if and when he wishes, no matter how little money he has, provided there is someone willing to sell it to him?
>
> (b) Should Freddy be allowed to buy a car on instalments if he has a history of unemployment, or if he has been on welfare?
>
> (c) If Freddy has been unemployed, or if he has been on welfare, should he be allowed to buy only certain kinds of cars? e.g. used cars?

---

* Two sources of these situations are: T. Altshuler, *Choices* (New York: Prentice-Hall, 1970), and K. J. Weber, *Prose of Relevance 1 and 2* (Toronto: Methuen Publications, 1971).

(d) What would your opinion of Freddy be if you knew that his wife had begged him not to buy the car?

(e) What would your opinion of Freddy's *purchase* be, if you knew that the used car dealership was in danger of going bankrupt?

(f) Was the salesman at the used car dealership just doing his job?

3. After the group discussion, each student compares *his* initial reaction with the group's.

Step Three: A variation of Step Two. Students are presented with a situation such as the one below. Instead of following prepared guidelines for discussion, *they* design the questions with which one might approach such a situation.

> You completely forget to do a very important assignment. Anyone who fails to hand it in on the appointed day could fail the term. Fortunately it is on mathematics problems and can be copied quickly. You borrow a friend's assignment at lunch and copy it. An hour later in mathematics class, the teacher is collecting the work when you realize that you have your own copied version, but you have lost your friend's original one. He sits in the desk beside yours. What do you do?

For further work in Step Three, students can devise and write situations such as the one above.

Step Four: Critical analysis of persuasive prose. All journals encourage controversy, even the most respected. Unfortunately for adolescent slower learners, the most respected journals which always insist on accuracy and documentation for any polemic they present, are at the same time the most difficult to read. For this reason and for reasons of social orientation, adolescent slower learners are more likely to read the polemics of a journal or newspaper which takes less care in its arguments, its research, and its presentation. The attitude with which a relatively uninformed person approaches this kind of prose is important. Hence, teaching critical awareness — literally teaching how to ask questions — should occupy a significant part of the cognitive curriculum.

The exercise that follows is an example of the kind of material that can help to foster critical awareness.

139

Marriage

Of all the long-standing and sacred ideas that are dying in the twentieth century, the one that should disappear more than any other, is the traditional concept of marriage.

In the early days of man's existence, marriage developed as a device to guarantee the safety and security of women. Kings and governments supported the institution for it ensured that the nation would continue in an orderly way. Also, married couples made for a much more subdued population. Churchmen, too, supported the idea of marriage because it made people easier to control. Eventually, social custom, by frowning upon illegitimacy and bachelorhood — even by questioning whether bachelorhood was moral let alone desirable — made marriage the ultimate goal of every child of both sexes.

But in the culture of the twentieth century these factors no longer apply. Consequently, marriage as we know it, is out of date. Bachelorhood and illegitimacy are no longer such undesirable states. Governments, by gradually relaxing divorce laws, seem to be admitting that perhaps marriage may not be so stable after all. And certainly, women with equal opportunities and jobs, no longer need marriage for security.

Marriage, therefore, is a holdover from earlier times, kept alive chiefly by women who find it a convenient social comfort.

1. Examine the article carefully for any instances of false or questionable reasoning.

2. This analysis ignores several major factors about marriage. What are they?

3. Why would rulers consider marriage a stabilizing feature in a nation? Why would churchmen?

4. Use the last paragraph as subject for a debate.

There are many more approaches to teaching slower learners the importance of a sound critical faculty. And this fact is true as well of creative and logical thinking. The key factor is simply *that it be done.* A cognitive curriculum, while it is only part of the adolescent slower learner's total program can nevertheless be the vanguard of all those techniques a teacher may muster to break through the dense fog of negativism that these students develop so relentlessly throughout their schooling. Adolescent slower learners *can* think. And if all that the cognitive curriculum manages to do is to make them realize this fact, then that in itself is sufficient.

USEFUL BOOKS

Covington, M. V. "Productive Thinking and a Cognitive Curriculum". Invited paper presented at symposium *Studies of the Inquiry Process: Problems of Theory, Description and Teaching.* Washington D.C.: American Psychological Association Convention, September, 1967.

Cox, R. and Unks, N. *A Selected and Annotated Bibliography of Studies Concerning the Taxonomy of Educational Objectives: Cognitive Domain.* University of Pittsburgh: Learning Research and Development Center, June, 1967.

Crutchfield, R. S. "Nurturing the cognitive skills of productive thinking". 1969 Yearbook, Association for Supervision and Curriculum Development.

Osborne, A. F. *Applied Imagination.* New York: Charles Scribner's Sons, 1953.

Parnes, S. J. *Creative Behaviour Guidebook.* New York: Charles Scribner's Sons, 1967.

Parnes, S. J. *Creative Behaviour Workbook.* New York: Charles Scribner's Sons, 1967.

Parnes, S. J. *Creativity: Unlocking Human Potential.* Buffalo, N.Y.: The Creative Education Foundation, 1972.

Supplementary Guide to *Applied Imagination.* Buffalo N.Y.: The Creative Education Foundation.

Puzzle Solutions

Never give students problems which you have not first attempted yourself.

Note that most puzzles have more than one possible solution.

Creativity Section

Step One

1.

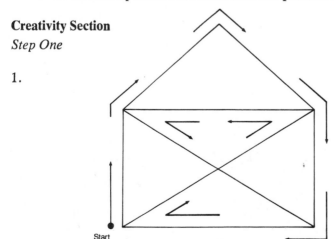

Start

2.

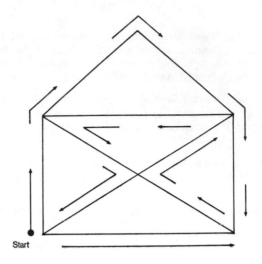

Start

3.

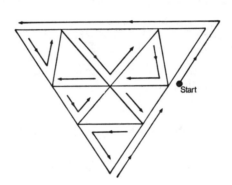

Start

4.

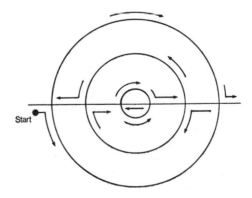

Start

Step Two

1. The *friend* must have been the *mother*.
2. Three generations of the same family.
3. Neither. They will be the same distance when they meet.
4.
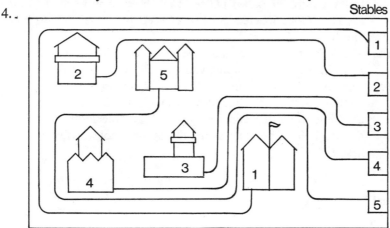
5. The thirteenth day. At the twelve foot level it climbs four feet and is *out*.
6. Fill the 5 gallon measure. From it fill the three. This leaves two gallons in the five. Empty the three and pour the two gallons into it. Fill the five. Pour from it into the three. Since the three will hold only one more gallon, you are left with four gallons in the five gallon measure.

Step Three

1. The bee flew a steady 70 m.p.h. for one hour. Hence it travelled 70 miles.
2.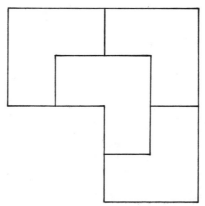

Step Four

(many possible solutions)

2. (a) The *trainee pilot* flies until he sees the lights of a town, then turns on his landing lights and flies in small circles. The air traffic controller radios police in all the nearby towns to watch for this. Once located, an experienced pilot flies out to guide him in.

    (b) The *hollow cylinder* contains water because it has been leaking. Heat it; watch for escaping vapour, and weld the leak.

    (c) The *Eskimos* hunt in pairs. They walk one immediately behind another, putting their feet down as with *one* footstep. One stops at a hole; the other continues — with audible footsteps — to a nearby hole. The seals avoid the second hole in favor of the first and . . . .

Logical Thinking

Step One

(a) 16
     35
     12

(b) eleven minutes

Step Two

Two prisoners cross. One returns and gets the third prisoner. He brings the boat back, gets out, and two soldiers cross. Then a soldier and a prisoner return. The prisoner gets out and the remaining soldier gets in. Both soldiers cross, get out, and the one prisoner who is across gets in, and in two trips, brings the other two prisoners across.

144

CHAPTER TEN

Encouraging Appreciation

Think of it, *Hamlet* in twelve pages! *In prose!* The mere thought that such a publication exists, is enough to raise the gorge of any English teacher. But to see it being taught as a substitute for the real thing is grounds for homicide in the name of literary integrity!

The thought of action at least that drastic occurred to me when I once saw just such material being used at a school for adolescent slower learners. The school had extended an invitation to come, observe, and comment, and the Hamlet lesson was the first I was to see. The students were the equivalent of tenth grade in age, but not in accomplishment; yet their responses seemed accurate enough. And their perplexed, somewhat sceptical view of Hamlet's course of action seemed fairly typical of that age group. But *Hamlet* in prose had no soliloquies, no poetry, no humor, and no tragedy. As I sat at the back of the classroom, my mind groped for the words of condemnation that would govern my report. Yet before that report could be written, fortunately, I was to have yet another dramatic experience in the eternal search to understand the adolescent slower learner.

Whenever I am asked to observe a particular school's program for adolescent slower learners, I invariably adopt a somewhat eccentric, but very reliable research technique: board a bus with the students at the end of a day, sit there, and listen. On *"Hamlet*-day" my ears at first picked up the standard patter: who did what to whom and when; who planned to do what to whom, and when. And who would do what to whom if the plan did not work; all of this related of course, to the students' one common, shared experience — school, and all of it underlined by the usual shouts, shrieks, and flying objects.

About a mile from the school, the topic of conversation changed. The bus had stopped to pick up a contingent of students from a highly respected, completely academic secondary school. Suddenly, the slower learners' patter switched to discussion of *Hamlet* — in overly loud tones. Comments on Gertrude, Ophelia, Laertes (usually pronounced *Lertis*) were bandied back and forth — not in the terms that grace *The English Quarterly,* but they *were* talking about *Hamlet,* and wanted to make that fact obvious!

With some amusement, and not a little sadness, I realized that the slower learners were trying to impress their academic — and to them, superior — colleagues! They wanted to show that they were students just like anyone else, that the "dummies", the "freaks", too, could wax intellectual.

Is this reason enough for teaching literature to slower learners? Does this justify watered-down summaries of Shakespearean plays, of classic novels? Probably the response to this lies more in an analysis of western culture than it does in a critical view of the slower learners' curriculum. But still an inescapable issue is whether or not the classics should be tampered with, whether or not injustice to a famous writer can be countenanced, in order to make slower learners *feel* better, to make them feel that they are getting as "good" an education as everyone else. Whenever I have posed the question to colleagues whose experience is chiefly at university level, the response is invariably a firm negative. To the practicing teachers of the adolescent slower learner, however, the question is not so clear-cut. Most often, the response is an honest, if somewhat embarrassed "If it *works,* then well . . . ".

"If It Works . . ."

Too often the reason given by practicing teachers for teaching diluted literature is based solely on the vague notion of whether or not it "works". In fact that same notion is applied to almost anything the slower learner is taught. That something "works" in the classroom is a mystical concept used and understood it seems, only by teachers. When a lesson has "worked" it usually means that students have shown interest, have reacted to a greater or lesser degree, and that — especially in the case of slower learners — they have behaved in an acceptable manner. Unfortunately, there is rarely any evidence that cognitive or perceptive or affective growth has occurred among the students in a lesson that has "worked". All too frequently the term simply means that the lesson has worked for the teacher!

The reasons for presenting literature to adolescent slower learners must be more specific. Only if a teacher knows *why* he is teaching literature to these students are they likely to gain anything from it. A diluted, prose-summary *Hamlet* smacks more of an objective born of desperation, than it does of anything else. Yet as the teacher of that particular *Hamlet* class said to me with a shrug of his shoulders, "What's a teacher going to do?"

What *Is* A Teacher Going To Do?

A first step might be simply to ponder the question: Why teach *literature* to *adolescent slower learners?* And surely part of the answer must lie in those reasons for which we present literature to anyone: for enjoyment; for stimulation; for vicarious experience; to broaden horizons; because it is liberating, etc. One could argue too, that with slower learners the need is all the more profound because of their invariably narrow outlook. Yet over these refreshing and exciting reasons, the apparent reality of the slower learner classroom hangs like a ponderous cloud of doom. No matter how broadening the experience of Hawthorne's *The Scarlet Letter* may be, the majority of adolescent slower learners will not like it and will probably reject it. No matter how exciting Dickens' *A Tale of Two Cities* may be, they will not read it. And no matter how fascinating *Othello* is as a study of man, they will not understand it. Now, what is a teacher to do?

Take a leaf from the book of common sense. Those people who love literature have grown to that state over a long period of time. Slower learners are not likely to reach that state in one leap either — assuming of course that they will, or must, reach it ever. A student who does not read at all because he sees no relevance in what he is reading, is not likely to change that conviction when he is presented with *Jane Eyre*. But he *may* consent to reading *Nurse Jane's Last Stand**, if only because the immediate gratification suggested by such a title may seem appealing. This is not to denigrate the classics. Surely the comprehension and enjoyment of *Jane Eyre* should be an objective, but how can a student's reading be improved, his appreciation of literature be encouraged if he will not read *at all*? What a teacher "is to do" is to begin where the students *are*, not where he thinks they should be.

What this means in courses where appreciation is an objective, is that teachers must adjust their curricular sights — and not in the direction of diluted abridgements either. It may well be that their students throughout the course of their school careers may never grow to the stage of reading and enjoying great literature. But unless those students are reading and appreciating *something* — be it only *Nurse Jane's Last Stand* — by the time they leave school, the fact that they will *never* read the classics is an absolute certainty.†

Teaching "Second-Level" Literature

Fortunately, many publishers today are providing an abundance of reading material, usually paperback novels, that fill the gap between "great" literature and nothing at all. And these novels are not second rate. Usually they are interesting, highly relevant pieces that are reflections of

---

* The hyperbole is my invention. If the title does exist somewhere, my apologies to the author. KJW.

† I have met a few teachers whose dedicated and near-evangelical conviction about great literature has inspired even the slowest of slower learners. God bless and preserve them for they are indeed rare.

the contemporary scene. Naturally, their impact is shortlived, because they are concerned with immediate issues and situations. This is probably one of the major factors that precludes their becoming classics. But as these titles disappear, they are replaced again and again with printings of new novels.*

For the classroom teacher who decides to utilize these second level novels, there must be a change in the traditional approach and emphasis. Because a classic — say *Jane Eyre* — has so much to discuss and appreciate and enjoy, an English class may spend up to six weeks "taking" it. On the other hand, a title from second-level literature may provide only *one* feature of great writing — perhaps an exciting plot, or maybe character delineation, or fantasy, or setting, or conflict. To give one of these titles the same time as *Jane Eyre* is unfair to the teacher, the students, and the book. If six weeks are allotted for the novel study and in the teacher's best opinion, this amount of time is necessary, then why not study five or even six second-level novels, each of which provides at least one different example of all those features found together in *Jane Eyre* — which the students will not read.

Even in novels of the second level, a teacher can still seek the objectives of enjoyment, stimulation, vicarious experience, broadening, liberation . . . . And if this is what the students will read, then it makes sense to begin there.

All Right. If We Accept Second-Level Novels, There Is Still The Problem Of Getting Slower Learners To Read Them

An earlier chapter has already suggested an approach to the novel which experience has shown to be very useful. That technique recognizes the varying levels of ability in a slower learner class and accommodates that fact by providing several titles of varying difficulty, but on a common theme. However there are situations where for whatever reason, the class must all read and study the same novel. When such situations occur, the inevitable outcome after two or three days of assigned reading is that one or two students have finished the whole book. Some are on page 83. Some are on page 7 and a few have yet to begin!

To combat this syndrome, a teacher can take advantage of two factors: the first, that second-level novels are usually very interesting, and the second, that almost every student, even the most sophisticated,

---

* There are of course, many classics, many titles of the "first-level" which slower learners will read most willingly, such as Salinger's *The Catcher In The Rye,* Steinbeck's *Of Mice and Men,* etc.

enjoys being read to. Therefore, before studying the novel, if the teacher reads to the slower learner class for two or even three consecutive periods of class time, with the students following in their books, the whole class together can be helped over the "hump" of interest and be literally led into the world of that novel. Once the students are well into the story, completing it on their own is an easier and even welcome assignment. This particular method, too, enables the teacher and class to discuss the novel later as a whole entity, eliminating the need to go through it chapter by chapter, a time-consuming, onerous approach.

When every member of a slower learner class — or *almost* every member, given a typical class — has read the whole novel before discussing it, the teaching-learning situation is more rewarding, for the class has a common shared experience to which they may commit themselves. From this point, a teacher can guide a class of slower learners through the novel by whatever method he deems appropriate or desirable.

As For Poetry

Manuelo came to Canada from Puerto Rico in January. Whatever culture shock he may have felt was compounded by the fact that his family had chosen to emigrate during one of the worst Canadian winters in years. One morning in late March, a day so cold that the windows in my classroom were frozen shut, Manuelo wrote this.

Dafodil (sic)

A dafodil is a chalice
Held up in spring.
To show that God
In winter
Is not dead
But only asleep.

And Manuelo was not the only budding poet in this particular class of adolescent slower learners. This piece was written by Brett, aged 14.

Truth

The wind blows in December,
Holding the truth
For you to feel.
And if your shelter walls
Are thick —
Forget the truth.
It's lost to you.

Carrie, aged 12, wrote this.

An Ancient Prison

What do you think Old Man,
As you sit there?
You are a prison
   In yourself.
Your canes are bars.
Your white hair is a badge
That marks you like a number.
Only your twisting
Stiff old fingers,
Show that there is something still inside you
That wants out.

These are by no means examples of great poetry. One might argue that they are hardly poetry at all. But they are a clear demonstration of an indisputable fact: adolescent slower learners can *feel*. They are as capable of sensitivity and emotion as any of their more successful colleagues. And very often their sensitivity is even greater, or at least more honest, for slower learners react to poetry with a kind of unsophisticated candor that differs from the reaction of their academic colleagues who all too often express only what they are *supposed* to feel.

Why then, if slower learners are capable of emotion and feeling, do they so frequently gain a reputation as poetry-haters?

"Why d'we have to do this stuff?"
"Pomes is for queers!"
"Why don't he say what he *means*?"
"Do we got to memorize this?"

In the first place there is the old problem of teacher and student expectation. The students feel they *must* react negatively to poetry. It is expected of them. And no teacher is surprised when it happens for he expects it too. This situation is then met with poetry which is guaranteed to make permanent those negative feelings. Titles like *Vigorous Verse, Poems for Boys, Poems for Girls** are introduced on the assumption that because adolescent slower learners are incapable of subtle feelings, they should therefore be given only rugged narratives. Since any kind of feeling is difficult with such poetry, everyone's expectations are confirmed, and the poetry-hating cycle is established.

---

* Again I have made these up. If the titles exist, my apologies.

Encouraging Appreciation and Sensitivity Through Writing Poetry

To many an adolescent slower learner, there are two worlds — his own, and everything else "out there". For a class or even a single student in whom the poetry-hating cycle is well-established, poetry is rejected simply because it is a creation of the "other" world. But since slower learners can feel, since they have words and ideas, it seems reasonable that they can be drawn to poetry by first trying to write some themselves. In other words, by writing their own poetry, slower learners realize that the supposed barrier between their own world, and the "other" one does not really exist. Writing poetry then is a first stage in encouraging appreciation and sensitivity.

A Few Practical Ideas*

1. **The Cinquain**

   This *five-line* poem combines words and parts of speech. It does not have to rhyme.

   Use the following pattern:
   Line 1: One word which is also the title.
   Line 2: *Two* words, both of which are *descriptive* words describing the title.
   Line 3: *Three* words, all *verbs,* which describe the typical actions of your subject.
   Line 4: A *four*-word *phrase* describing your emotion about your subject.
   Line 5: *One* word which can either be a repetition of line 1 or a synonym of that line.

   Examples:

Ice-cream	Crowds
smooth, cold	loud, rough
melting, soothing, sticking	shoving, cheering, fighting
I love the taste	a mass of faces
Ice-cream	Hordes

2. **The Image Couplet**

   This "poem" contains only two lines.
   (a) The first line consists of an image taken from everyday life:
     (i) A soldier firing his gun;
     (ii) A skywriter's trail zig-zagging across the sky.

---

* Two outstanding books on this topic have been written by Brian Powell. See footnote page 50.

(b) The second line expands this image by comparing it to something similar but unrelated. (Try to see connections between completely unrelated things.)

   (i) A soldier firing his gun,
      A lizard shooting out its tongue.

  (ii) A skywriter's trail zig-zagging across the sky,
      A beetle dragging crumbs across the sand.

3. The Syllable Poem

This poem consist of *nine* lines and is based on a number of syllables per line.

Line 1: contains 1 syllable   —
Line 2: contains 2 syllables   — —
Line 3: contains 3 syllables   — — —
Line 4: contains 4 syllables   — — — —
Line 5: contains 5 syllables — — — — —
Line 6: contains 4 syllables   — — — —
Line 7: contains 3 syllables   — — —
Line 8: contains 2 syllables   — —
Line 9: contains 1 syllable   —

Each line may contain only one word, or several words that comprise the required number of syllables. Each word should somehow relate back to the title.

Example:

Insect	Desert
fly	hot
buzzing	lifeless
round and round	unearthly
stop, creep, stop, sprint	ever-stretching
sit up. look. wring hands.	vegetationless
more creep. more stop.	ever-silent
closer. wait.	motionless
closer.	wasteful
swat!	sand

Further Activity In Word Awareness And Sensitivity

4. Make a list of brand names which seem especially alliterative.

5. Write down and scan a counting-out rhyme or skip-rope you once chanted.

6. Make a list of 8 concrete details, each of which serves as an example of *one* of the following:

   (a) amusement park smells
   (b) circus colors
   (c) sounds of a locker room
   (d) the feel of things barefoot in the dark
   (e) the contents of a lady's purse or a little boy's pocket
   (f) what a goat might smell as he passes by a dump
   (g) the odors encountered on a walk through a department store
   (h) early morning sounds

7. Advertisers deliberately create names for their products which connote cleanliness, elegance, excitement, etc. Choosing a single line of goods (such as "cars" in the example below) try to determine which "virtue" the names of the items collectively suggest.

   Example:
   Fury, Mustang, Dart, Sting-ray, Barracuda, and Meteor all connote explosive energy.

8. Draw a word so that it looks like what it says.

   Example:
   corn   incomplet   m
    e   bu p
    r

9. Create a two-column menu in which both columns list exactly the same fare, but in which one column describes the food with fancier, richer, more favorably connotative names than the other.

   Example:

cold crab meat	iced cocktail of imported king crab
potatoes with cheese	creamed potatoes au gratin
chopped beef	salisbury steak au jus
mixed chocolate and	fudge ripple supreme
vanilla ice-cream	

10. Other methods include the teaching of Haiku.

    The sky is dark and dreary
    The ocean lies still
    A gull flies over.

    Carolyn, aged 12.

Yes, They Can!

It's all yellow
Wet and noise
When a chick is born.

Pat, aged 6.

A car drives fast
Soon, a terrible scream,
There. The car stops.

Manuela, aged 15.

Poetry Study With Adolescent Slower Learners

Once the students attempt to write poetry, no matter how ineffective or lacking in quality their efforts may be, it is a relatively simple task to lead them to the appreciation and discussion of more professional writing. A useful transition however, is to study a few poems written by other students, poems which for one reason or another have some significant merit. For example:

On the Way to School*

On the way to school
One morning long ago
I stopped to look
At the sunrise
I looked too long
I missed my bus
I failed school
I got a crumby job
I spent my life
Looking at sunrises
And sunsets
I lived in poverty
And died rich.

Ron Sedor, Thunder Bay, Ontario

When Ron Sedor's reflection on school is discussed *first,* a move to William Blake's "The Schoolboy" or Wordsworth's "The Tables Turned" is not only painless, but exciting.

Equally interesting is the approach to poetry in combination with contemporary popular song. Using both the music and the lyrics to

---

* Published in *Truth & Fantasy* (Methuen Publications, 1972.)

popular songs — many of which are beautiful poetry in their own right — a class can lead then to poetry of a similar theme.

Once students enjoy poetry, the choice of pieces to be discussed and classroom techniques to be used are limited only to the ingenuity applied.

And Drama?

There is an ancient proverb very popular today in teacher training colleges:

> I remember nothing of what I hear,
> And half of what I see,
> But all of what I do.

For adolescent slower learners, there is some justification in adding a second stanza.

> We appreciate little of what we hear,
> And only some of what we see,
> But when we *do* something : . .!

Developmental — or creative — or improvisational drama — whatever name is applied — is a tremendously positive force for a class of adolescent slower learners. A carefully designed program in developmental drama, one that builds slowly, one that is geared to developing confidence and self-expression, can accomplish a great deal in fulfilling a slower learner's emotional needs. Through acting out a situation, whether it is a planned or a spur-of-the-moment idea, a slower learner gets outside himself to see what others see of him. He also has a chance to *act out,* to burn off those hostilities that so often simmer inside him. And by assuming the role or character of an imagined person, he has an opportunity to express himself without the embarrassments and insecurities that keep him from self-expression at other times. Role playing develops sensitivity to other people. It develops awareness and trust. In fact, it is the totality of the technique that makes developmental drama so effective for adolescent slower learners.

Why then is it not more popular? Probably because it is far removed from traditional classroom techniques. There are no notes, few books, little concrete evidence of remediation. It is difficult to test (a shoal on which has foundered many a creative idea). And it makes noise.

As well there are limited means for convincing the detractors of developmental drama that the technique may have merit. Picture for example, a rigidly conservative teacher peering through a classroom door at a class of adolescent slower learners doing a "warm up" exercise. Let us say that they are "being seaweeds". The students are preparing themselves mentally and physically for participation in a dramatic situation. But all that the sceptical teacher sees is a group of students waving back and forth in answer to some kind of destructive mania!

Developmental drama really cannot be argued. It has to be experienced. Only those teachers who have watched their slower learners be literally transformed, are capable of understanding its real value.

Sample Situation

To give a complete explanation of a program in developmental drama, its principles, its implementation, etc., is quite beyond the intended scope of *Yes, They Can!* However, at the end of this chapter, there are listed five titles, which taken together would provide an excellent foundation for such a program. The sample situation that follows can be most effectively used after a program is fairly well along, but in the hands of a creative teacher it might be attempted without much advance preparation.

This situation provides wide scope for dramatic improvisation. At the same time it can be used for oral work, creative thinking, critical analysis, writing of drama, short story writing, debate, etc.

The Beginning

A nuclear war has just ended. Most of the civilized world has been obliterated. Although the war is over, there is now a very high radiation count. Only high winds, rain, and time can lower the count, and make the world habitable again.

In a fallout shelter, the following people have sought refuge. The shelter was designed for four people, but if supplies are carefully watched, six people might live for as long as five months.

Mr. Ward: 63 years old. A successful businessman. He has been an active community organizer for years. Rather a grandfatherly type of person.

Zack Osant: 22 years old, a drifter. He left his parents at age 15, held a variety of jobs. The most successful job he has ever had was as a drummer in a rock band. He writes poetry.

Doris Angel: 23 years old, very attractive, healthy, athletic. She is a former physical education teacher. Very much aware of her charms, she is not above using them to get her own way.

Davis Bass: 31 years old, pleasant, ordinary fellow. He had worked as a dispatcher for a large trucking company. The father of two children who were killed in the first minutes of the war.

Freda Bass: 30 years old, David's wife. She is quiet, unassuming, but loves her husband dearly. She is seven months pregnant.

Tom Kander: 24, strong, healthy, a diesel mechanic. Although he has only grade eight education, he is very intelligent. He is brooding and sullen. He is an Indian.

Parker Mendoran: 28-year-old minister who had spent most of his career working with slum children. He is friendly, personable. People instinctively trust him. He is a severe epileptic, but controls his seizures with a drug.

Honora Kenton: 30, and a registered nurse. She is rather plain, but very intelligent, and very nervous.

April Seaton: 32, career woman. She had been a highly successful dress designer, and had expanded her business to such a size that most of her recent work was purely administrative. She is intelligent and vicious. She hates men.

Jacques Valleau: 25, law student, strong, healthy and handsome. Proud of his French-Canadian heritage, he had been planning to enter the firm of his wealthy father in Montreal.

Peter Dallas: 26, advertising executive. He had been very successful. Unmarried because of an admitted "roving-eye".

Lois Dexter: 51, no children, widowed in first hour of the war. High-strung, bossy, spoiled. She owns the shelter.

Situations like the one above are relatively simple to devise. Some of the best, in my experience, have been invented, designed and written by slower learning students in creative thinking sessions. For example, the following situation, less involved than *The Beginning,* but equally dramatic, was the creation of Judi, aged 14 (with spelling corrected).

In the Canadian North, a bush pilot makes an emergency landing in a blizzard, while attempting to rescue two men. One man is an Indian guide and father of seven children; the other is a wealthy, childless geologist, middle-aged. Both men have diphtheria. Because of the weather, the crashlanding is unsuccessful. The pilot is saved but everything is destroyed except one vial of serum, enough for *one* of the men. The radio is working and the pilot calls for instructions.

Roles:
We never see the pilot or the men. We see only the office of the emergency centre. In it are the geologist's wife, the Indian's wife and one of her children, the radio operator, and a doctor. The serum must be injected within the next hour.

(Judi's situation was so well received by her classmates that it was eventually scripted and performed as part of the school's annual Talent Show.)

USEFUL BOOKS

Frazier, C., and Meyer, A. *Discovery in Drama*. New York: The Paulist Press, 1969. Originally developed for Christian education; it presents many topical issues for classroom use; not an elementary text.

Hodgson, J., and Richard, E. *Improvisation*. London: Methuen, 1966. A very good compendium of ideas; very well structured; makes haste slowly.

McCasin, N. *Creative Dramatics In the Classroom*. New York: David McKay, 1968. A fairly simple text containing a wide variety of interesting ideas.

Siks, G. B. *Creative Dramatics*. New York: Harper and Row, 1958. Geared to younger children; particularly good for philosophy.

Spolin, V. *Improvisation For the Theatre*. Northwestern University Press, 1963. An excellent text, and a necessary part of any bibliography; contains long lists of ideas, practical suggestions, do's and don't's.

CHAPTER ELEVEN

Using Popular Media* to Develop Awareness

The Newspaper

The pages that follow outline three different uses of the newspaper that have proven to be effective with slower learners. Ideally, each of the three kinds of activities would not be treated consecutively, but at different points throughout a school year.

I
General Reading and Perception Activity

1. **Reading Comprehension:**

   Ideal because of contemporary aspect and relevancy of "news". An interesting project which requires some advance preparation by the teacher is to have small groups prepare summaries of the front page stories. (A group is given a particular story and asked to reduce it to its 4 or 5 or 6 *main points.*)

2. **Using Editorial and Opinion Columns:**
   (a) Bracket or underline the *facts* in these articles.
   (b) Select biased words or expressions.
   (c) A third exercise requires more advance preparation. Prepare a series of questions which elicit *judgment* responses from the students. They are asked questions about the opinion of the editorial writer, the soundness of his stand, the means by which he argues, etc.

3. **Personal Advice Columns:**

   Letters provide the basis for a short story; for a section of dialogue; for a report, etc.

4. **Want Ads:**
   (a) Students can respond to certain ads by writing letters of applica-cation, although it is not wise to spend too much time on this.

---

* This chapter has deliberately omitted advertising and film. Advertising, I have found, is such a popular subject with teachers of younger children that for adolescents it is often redundant. The teaching of film is so well treated in so many books that further work is unnecessary here — except perhaps to note my observation that in recent years many schools which use film seem to be using it so indiscriminately that it is losing its effect for adolescent slower learners. Using film as a desperate safety valve, or as a substitute for teaching is not good pedagogy. (KJW)

(b) An interesting exercise grows out of *ad preparation*. Students are to sell an article with an ad prepared at minimum cost. For instance, the first ten words cost 10¢ a piece, next ten cost 20¢, next ten cost 50¢ . . . .

(c) A creative exercise: after reading the personal columns with all the codes, and come-home pleas, have students prepare the most unusual possible personal ad.

5. **Letters to the Editor:**
   (a) Have students write letters to the editor. Newspapers print an amazingly high percentage of student letters, *provided* the letters deal with issues that are really of students' concerns, e.g., "A developer is building on a vacant lot, and now we have to play on the street."
   (b) Examine letters to the editor for logic. Follow the thought process, and mount arguments in response, pointing out flaws.

6. **Headlines:**
   (a) Before reading the news stories that follow certain headlines, have students write a brief description of these headlines, outlining what the headlines suggest will follow. (These headlines are selected by the teacher in advance, usually stories from the inside pages which describe an unusual event or a hitherto unknown local issue.)
   (b) Have students prepare headlines for any short stories or narratives they have written. They must follow typesetting restrictions: say, for instance, the headline may have a total of not less than 30 or more than 40 *letters,* including spaces.

7. **Photographs:**
   (a) Analyze photographs *without* the caption to assess their impact.
   (b) What effect does the caption have?
   (c) If students are capable, try some photojournalism exercises. Using a polaroid camera, take some pictures of a situation which could take place in the classroom — broken window, argument, something escapes in biology lab — etc. One group describes the situation merely by observing and being aware of it. Another group is kept from knowing the situation, but describes what happened after they see the pictures. Compare the results.

8. **Advertising:**
   If it is possible to get a set of newspapers from a town or city that is

quite some distance away, the following activity helps students' perception a great deal.

Students examine the out-of-town newspaper's advertising but *do not* read any news stories. Strictly by virtue of reading and looking at the advertisements, they are to determine the nature of the community served by this newspaper. It is usually a good idea to provide the students with guide questions such as:

> Is the community large? How do you know?
> Is it predominantly rural, or urban?
> Is it a wealthy community?
> What are some of the favorite recreational activities?
> Is there a lot of do-it-yourself activity?
> What does this tell you?
> Are there Boutiques? What does this mean?

9. **Editorial Page Cartoon:**
   (a) For teaching parody and satire. (The concepts are more important than the definitions.)
   (b) Valuable in teaching the idea of the newspaper as The Fourth Estate.

II
Teaching The Newspaper As A Specific Genre

Stage One:

It is important to establish the newspaper as a living, exciting organism. This might be done by taking students to the library for research into newspaper history. (The first known daily: Acta Diurna, Rome, 69 B.C.)

A technique that rarely fails is to bring in many out-of-town dailies, a fairly broad representation. Also bring in some underground papers.

Stage Two:

Bring to class a set of the newspaper that is to be studied. Allow students to peruse but leave them with this homework assignment. Select any one news story that begins on the front page and answer these questions:
1. Who? What? When? Where?
2. Why?
3. In the story itself, mark the point at which each of these questions were answered. Hopefully, students will discover the journalistic principle of the inverted triangle — all questions are answered at the beginning and elaboration follows.

Stage Three:
Take up homework. Discuss inverted triangle.

Stage Four:
Using the same issue of the newspaper, break down the news section into world, local, human interest.

Examine how the paper has given *emphasis* on the front page with headline, proportion, type-size, placement on the page.

Stage Five:
Study the editorial section using the following suggestions as a guide.

1. What are the *topics* of the editorials? Where does the paper stand on these issues?

2. Bring to class copies of one week's issue of the paper (five copies of Monday's issue, five of Tuesday, etc.). Break class into groups and have each group make a chart of the issues treated on the editorial page, e.g., Topic _____; Paper's opinion of this topic _____.

   Note the findings of each group, and try to come to some conclusion about the paper's editorial policy.

Stage Six:
Keep the same groups and the same copies of the paper. Make a similar chart for the letters to the editor.

What kinds of people read this paper?

Stage Seven:
Using the same groups and the same copies, examine all the columnists in the news and editorial sections (not the sports or entertainment or business columnists).

By looking at a week's issues in groups you should be able to answer the following questions:

1. In what ways is a columnist different from a reporter?
2. Do any of the columnists have particularly strong views?
3. Does the paper have columnists with opposing views?
4. Why do papers have columnists?

Stage Eight:
Stages Two, Three and Four can be repeated in whole, in part, or in variation, for the business, sports, entertainment and family sections. It is usually a good idea to bring in new copies at this point.

Stage Nine:

Discuss whether or not this paper considers itself strictly a community organ, or does it have a wider horizon?

What does it add to the community?

III
Writing A Newspaper In Class
Stage One:

Choice of an editor-in-chief, and editors of the sections to be covered (usually world, local, business, sports, entertainment, family). The editor-in-chief presides over the editorial page, and over the layout of the front page, choosing how much space is given to world, local and "hot" news.

Stage Two:

Editors decide the nature and style of the newspaper. (Do not allow this to become a complex aspect.)

Stage Three:

Writing. Usually the procedure is smoothest if the teacher *appoints* the people who are to write in the various newspaper sections.

The following breakdown suggests a list of thirty possible topics.

Sample Breakdown
(assuming a class of 30)

World News Section and Local News Section

1. Editor — writes article on a development in a tense world crisis
2. World news — state of an ongoing crisis
3. "Hot" front page item — a natural disaster
4. Local news — accident at Pharmacy Street and St. Clair Street
5. Local news — report on construction
6. Report of a charity campaign

Entertainment

7. Editor — article on *trends* in television programming
8. Television review — review of any television program
9. Movie review — review of recent movie by columnist
10. Assembly — review of recent assembly
11. School dance — review

Family Section

12. Editor — general trends in fashion
13. Article on a particular fashion trend
14. A fashion show report by a columnist

Sports Section

15. Editor — article on an organized league — football, hockey, baseball
16. Report on recent game
17. Sports editorial, e.g., what's happening to amateurs
18. School sports — report on a game
19. Editorial on school sports

Editorial Section

20. Editor — editorial on a specific aspect of curriculum
21. Editorial on aspect of school policy
22. Editorial on city, e.g., traffic
23. Editorial — school activities by a columnist
24. Editorial on construction (or current topic)
25. Letters to the editor

Business and Finance

26. Editor — article on job opportunities for students
27. Article on new shops in one of the local areas

Columnists

28. One on sports
29. One on teenage entertainment habits
30. One on popular topic

Stage Four:
Usually two periods of class time are adequate for writing the articles. The teacher at this time is a very busy resource person.
The next stages, *practically,* work best this way.
(a) Students prepare final copy on alternate lines.
(b) Each editor "copy edits" his own section.
(c) Teacher does final copy editing.
(d) Turn back to students for rewriting.
(e) Collect; editor-in-chief and editors work out layout with the school's typing classes.

Note that throughout the writing, the editor-in-chief and the editor must approve the *thesis* or basic idea of everything that is written.

One final tip. To include photographs and advertising makes this a very major project. It is best to avoid these the first time you "do" a newspaper.

Magazines

Teachers can do much to make adolescent slower learners realize that magazines are living things with personalities all their own.

Too often however, we take something which generates a natural interest and in the name of pedagogy, destroy it by doing a formal dissection analysis. To introduce the idea painlessly then, bring into a classroom as many copies of different magazines as possible. On the first day of the magazine probe, simply allow the students to browse. Let them talk, compare, trade; the only thing that is asked of them is that by the end of the period each of them will have selected *one* magazine on which he will become an expert.

On the following day, the students begin to probe their selection. This guide usually helps.

How is the magazine put together?
1. Is there a general group of people to whom the magazine appeals?
2. Do the articles support this appeal?
3. What is the magazine's editorial point of view?
4. What is the ratio of advertising to printed articles?
5. What is the general tone of the letters written to the editor?
6. What do the letters to the editor tell you about the readership?
7. What use is made of color? What kind of paper is used? Does the size of the paper make any difference?
8. (a) How much photography is used in relation to written copy?
   (b) Does this relationship vary from article to article?

What does the advertising tell you?
1. Who advertises in the magazine?
2. At whom are the ads directed?
3. What is the general appeal of the ads?
4. How are the ads structured?
   (a) color
   (b) humor
   (c) ratio of photography to copy

Yes, They Can!

Examine one or two magazines that compete for a similar readership

1. Is your magazine different? In what ways?
2. Why is the circulation of your magazine greater or less than its competitor?

The results of all this research can culminate in a written report, an oral report, or better still, panel or seminar discussions, especially for those who picked the more popular magazines with which everyone is likely to have at least a nodding acquaintance.

A natural step from here is to prepare a magazine in class. I have found that a system of small groups each producing a magazine is not as successful as pooling the talent of the entire class in the production of a major piece.

As a class, decide on a specific readership, and a type of magazine to appeal to that readership. The simplest formula to follow is something in the nature of *Time* or *Newsweek,* since there is a great deal of writing, not very much unusual photography, and relatively uncomplicated advertising. Then too, this type of magazine would satisfy the wants of everyone in the class. The selection of an appropriate name follows, along with a discussion of what type of articles should be written, the spirit of the advertising, etc.

An Editorial Advisory Board consists of the editor-in-chief and his assistant, the advertising editor, the features editor and his assistant. This in no way approximates a real magazine staff but it is efficient for the classroom, provided responsibilities are clearly defined. To each editor then, a group of students is assigned. Some are writing feature articles; others are preparing advertising copy. The whole class is involved.

As always, there are a few students whose work is completed well ahead of the rest of the class. They can write letters to the editor, prepare an advice column, or an "editor answers" column.

Rather than have a separate photography department (too much liaison and coordination involved) it is best to have a photographer attached to each group. "Instant" pictures are necessary, since they often affect the article that goes with them. Students can learn how image affects prose or vice versa, in magazine writing. Also, inappropriate photographs can be rejected and new ones taken immediately without waiting days for developing.

Usually, the magazine takes only three or four periods to complete, so that the entire writing project from beginning to end takes little more than a week.

Using Commercial Television For Study Units
Suggested Stages

1. In group discussions, have students analyze the reasons for the success of television, reasons why it has literally affected our entire culture. To what good use might mass televising be put? What are some of the obvious dangers?

2. Present on videotape a program from a half-hour series.
   This can be then analyzed in several ways.
   (a) Discuss the program as a short story.
   (b) Examine the features which affect the plot *because* it is a series.
   (c) What are the basic appeals of this particular program?
   (d) What are the inherent fallacies (if any)?

3. Repeat Stage 2, using as many different programs as desirable or feasible (soap opera, mystery, western).

4. The talk show phenomenon.
   (a) What are the features which give it success?

5. The game show phenomenon.
   (a) What are the features which give it success?
   (Note that Stages 4 and 5 can usually be covered in a single lesson, by taping small segments of each type of show, and showing them consecutively.)

6. It is quite useful to cover at least one series which has been critically regarded as consistently excellent.
   The American television series *Gunsmoke* has been successful internationally for over fifteen years. The brief guide below can be used as an aid in discussion.
   (a) *Basic set* of characters — easy identification.
   (b) Characters are fallible. Because the plot centres around someone *other* than the basic set, a happy outcome is not certain.
   (c) Basic set allows certain kinds of stereotyped interplay *anticipated* by the viewer.
   (d) Plot often presents serious moral or ethical issues and a pat solution is not guaranteed.
   (e) Appropriate music arranged for each show.
   (f) Deals with timeless subjects.
   (g) Realism in setting.

PART C

Four Footnotes
Based on Practical Experience

If this book has expressed a philosophy — other than my faith in the abilities of slower learners — it is that successful teaching is based on common sense. When adolescent slower learners are led to think and feel, it is not because of any one specific style of pedagogy, nor is it exclusively because of a curriculum, and it is not because of the structure and purpose of a specific school. Adolescent slower learners reach new insights when an intelligent teacher perceives the needs and recognizes the potential of those students. And there are many factors other than the act of teaching itself which lead to those insights.

Part C presents a brief outline of four of those factors: the need for a physical surrounding conducive to learning; recognition that adolescent slower learners *can* think; the importance of measuring progress; and the necessity of effective classroom management.

CHAPTER TWELVE

The Adolescent Slower Learner's Classroom: Contents and Appearance

The Case of ST4-10B

The biggest class I have ever taught went under the complex title of ST4-10B. They were not biggest in number, for there were only twenty-one in the group, but the size of each member of ST4-10B was enough to cow even the most confident instructor. All male. Average age seventeen. The average height and weight, I cannot remember. All I recall for certain is that they seemed huge.

To some extent, the reaction of a few of their teachers was predictable. In geography class, their sole activity was coloring maps. No discussion, no experimentation, no field excursions. Just coloring maps. Their science instructor forbade absolutely, the use of equipment. All required experiments she conducted herself, and the boys were told what observations to record. During physical education periods, their teacher would throw several basketballs into the gymnasium, retreat to his office, and lock the door.

Yet ST4-10B *never* did anything to justify this. There was the usual list of incomplete assignments, the usual unauthorized leave-taking; and they were often loud and boisterous. But aside from the fact that their collective appearance had all the threat of an impending hurricane, they never once did anything that could rightly be called a serious breach of propriety!

Strangely, the boys never complained about this treatment, accepting it all as a matter of course. That is, until they were forbidden use of the library. That was the turning point, the last straw. Not that ST4-10B exactly haunted the library. Usually any visits there were teacher-directed ones which they carried out with the same kind of lethargic acceptance that characterized the rest of their activity. But to be *forbidden* the library was more than they would tolerate. I expected revolt. At best some kind of collective revenge. Instead, what happened became a lesson for which I have never stopped being grateful.

Since English class was to them most closely associated with the library, the full weight of their righteous anger came down heavily on me, late one Friday afternoon. To my delighted — if wary — surprise however, their solution lay not in storming the library, but in forming one of their own! It was to be a library in which ST4-10B governed the choice of titles, in which their own form of book loan system would be established, and in which cataloguing and shelving would be carried out with complete informality.

Since my classroom was selected as the location of this library, I was quick to point out that there were no shelves, and that the school budget would probably preclude there being any built. On the following Monday morning, the back of my room was graced by a set of shelves the boys had made during the weekend (complete with a small, somewhat ineptly lettered plaque which said: *Donated by ST4-10B*).

The library was to be stocked entirely through donations and within a week over a hundred paperback titles were lining the shelves. However, the boys' resolve to govern the choice of titles quickly disappeared in favor of "we'll take anything". This was fortunate in a way, for the faculty's initial awe at ST4-10B's initiative was soon replaced by enthusiastic support. Once the teachers dipped into their personal collections, the ST4-10B Memorial Collection (sic!) began to grow. In three months, we had 1000 titles. In four months — the end of the year — there were over 2000 books — all at no cost to the school.

Admittedly, there were some repercussions and some drawbacks. The librarian resigned when the stock of books overflowed from my room into several adjacent classrooms*. The boys at first considered themselves guardians of their collection and were not only reluctant to share the books with students from other classes, but for a time did not want even their own classmates to take them off the shelves. Also, since the books were not censored, more than one unsavory title became part of the collection. In fact one morning I received a call from a parent who complained that his pornography collection had disappeared and I had better return it *fast*! (We were innocent.) And the loan system, which amounted to little more than "help yourself", made for countless missing books.

The benefits nevertheless, far outweighed the disadvantages. ST4-10B, with only a few exceptions, became avid readers. So did several other slower learner classes who used that room. But the real impact was in ST4-10B's attitude. To say that they became model students would be an exaggeration. Unknown to me, for example, ST4-10B had formed a committee at one point, to encourage donations. The committee, composed of the four biggest boys in the class, would single out some poor individual, and hovering over him, would point out the urgent need to increase the size of their library. Yet although they never became

---

* This librarian was an unfortunate exception to the members of that profession. I have never met a group of professional teachers with more dedication than librarians.

models of decorum, they did become models of spirit and high morale. Their positive outlook infused not only English class, but their other subjects as well. ST4-10B began to participate in school sports. They joined a few of the school clubs, and even made regular contributions to the school newspaper. And at the end of the year, ST4-10B went to the school principal and informed him that they were donating *their* library to the school!

Forming A Classroom Library: A Few Hints

1. Paperback books are the best material. They are inexpensive (therefore donatable"), appealing to students, and *available* in large quantity.
2. There should be no compunction, ever. Donations are on a voluntary basis. Loans are on an honor system.
3. Do *not* stamp books with the school crest or any insignia that indicates ownership.
4. Censorship should apply only insofar as the community would require it.
5. Use the books as a drawing card for adolescent slower learners. Discuss titles with them. Encourage them to make recommendations, critical comments. Above all, spend class time putting the library to good use.

Other Ideas For Bringing the Room to Life

1. Develop a "review board". On a small piece of paper a student writes the title of a book he has read. Underneath, he adds in a sentence or phrase some comment about the book. He then signs his name and posts the paper on the review board. This gives the teacher an opportunity to discuss a specific book with a specific student, and generates interest in a variety of titles.
2. Develop displays on bulletin boards and on walls of the classroom, but allow the students to do the creativity and the work.

   Divide a class or several classes into groups. Each group is responsible for a display which is to be kept for three weeks. Encourage the groups to develop their displays around a theme: advertising; nostalgia; teenage values; unusual headlines; acts of kindness; signs of the times.
3. Encourage slower learners to bring in and display the results of their craft options. For example, if a class of slower learners does wood working (or electronics, or plumbing, or metal work, or typing or commercial work or . . .) ask students to bring in a piece of their

work, a *small* piece, and display it along with a written description of how the piece was made.

4. An art class, or commercial art class can become part of a project in appreciation. The slower learner class selects specific haiku poems, or short poems of their own composition. They ask the art class to make visual representations of these in water colors or chalk. Hopefully, the slower learner class will communicate their specific wishes to the art class so that the experience will not only involve selecting a poem, but imagining, visualizing, and describing a setting for it.

5. Set aside a small section of display space for a "Let's Discuss It" board. The idea is that any student may bring in a newspaper clipping, a picture, or better still, write an account of some specific item which he would like to have discussed. This board, if properly promoted, can provide a considerable percentage of the material needed for a program in oral fluency. It often provides a safety valve for the hostility which otherwise would go unnoticed in slower learners until it expresses itself in some negative way. (ST4-10B's library began precisely on such a board.) Because there is a danger that it may become a complaint department, a teacher can enter things himself, hopefully things which help maintain a tone of reason and common sense.

6. Every teacher has at least a half dozen students with interesting hobbies. These too, make exciting displays, and generate discussion exercises, listening practice and subjects for creative thinking.

7. Posters, photographs, handbills, circulars, etc., also make interesting materials.

No matter what is used however, there are still two basic principles, both of them related to the fact that an interesting classroom makes for interested students. In the first place, no display should remain long enough to gather dust. After three weeks it becomes just another coat of paint. Secondly, displays should not be just *there;* they should be *used.* They should become a part of the curriculum.

An environment that is exciting in appearance, and that contains materials which students want and will use, is a classroom in which learning will take place. Dress it up! Sterility is for hospitals.

CHAPTER THIRTEEN

For Those Who Believe That Adolescent Slower Learners Cannot Think

The following project is not one of major proportion, but its results are of major significance to those who seek, sincerely, to understand and help the adolescent slower learner. It was conducted with a small class (J-11-12) at Don Head Secondary School* a vocational school for slower learning adolescents in Richmond Hill, Ontario. J-11-12 was a small group, because each of its members had demonstrated an even more serious lack of ability in the traditional pursuits than the typical slower learner. Jeannie for example could not quite master the 5x multiplication table. Sam, for some reason had a block about 6 x 7 and 7 x 6 — among other things. Angelo spoke only Italian at home and his results on English language reading tests were dismal. Freddie seemed to be unable to come to grips with his environment. He often did not seem to know where he was.

Each of the students in J-11-12, had been tested using the Wechsler Intelligence Scale for Children (WISC). Generally, those schools in Ontario which use the WISC tend to use the average of the Verbal Aptitude Score and the Performance Aptitude Score in determining student placement. If the average is approximately 80-85 or below, the student is considered a candidate for treatment as a slower learner.

Sam†	(age 15)	Verbal Apt.: 90	Performance Apt.: 87
Rick	(age 17)	V. A. 58	P. A. 82
Ashton	(age 15)	V. A. 72	P. A. 76
Angelo	(age 15)	V. A. 82	P. A. 80
Jeannie	(age 15)	V. A. 70	P. A. 86
Lorne	(age 15)	V. A. 62	P. A. 74
Freddie	(age 15)	V. A. 87	P. A. 90
Stuart	(age 15)	only average score available: 76	
Joseph	(age 15)	only average score available: 85	

In my course with them (I met them once a week) I emphasized

---

* An outstanding school in my opinion. At Don Head, the philosophy is one of kindness, flexibility, and mutual respect. All students, even the slowest, are given a sense of dignity and self-worth. There is no doubt in my mind, that this influenced the results.
† Unlike other first names in *Yes, They Can!*, these have been changed to avoid causing any embarrassment.

thinking for its own sake. Most of the material was built around problem and puzzle solving.

The results of this particular project are significant for two reasons: first, it is a clear demonstration that these adolescent slower learners — among the slowest in the school — could *think*. But perhaps what is ultimately more important is that the kind of thinking ability demonstrated in this little experiment was typical of their accomplishments — not at all unusual.

1. The project was carried out in one regular class period. The students were not told, nor were they led to suspect that any kind of testing or data gathering was taking place. To them it was a day like any other.

2. Five problems were presented (following). They were presented orally, and each problem involved objects that had to be manipulated in order to form certain shapes.

3. To aid their thinking, each student had objects at hand (small sticks, two inches in length) and they were encouraged to manipulate them in any way they wished.

4. Each problem was given a specific context. Rather than present them abstractly, I presented each problem as a concrete situation.

5. For each problem, the students began together. That is, each member of the class followed my instructions until the basic situation was established. Only after each of them had established the basic situation was the task presented.

The Problems:

1. Basic Situation.

"A farmer has three pigs which he keeps in triangular pens. The pens are made of gates and the gates are all the same length." (i.e. the sticks)

Task:

He can afford to buy one more pig, but he cannot afford more gates. Move the nine gates around until you make four pens that are all the same size.

2. Basic Situation.

"The farmer has been successful. He now has six pigs, and can afford *thirteen* gates. Each pig has its own pen, and the pens are all the same size. Here is how the farmer has penned his stock."

Task:

"One day there is an emergency. He needs a gate to replace a broken one at another place on the farm. This leaves only twelve gates for the pigs. Try to design six pens for the farmer, each of equal size, using only the twelve gates."

3. Basic Situation.

"The farmer also has six cows. These he keeps in square pens made of seventeen gates."

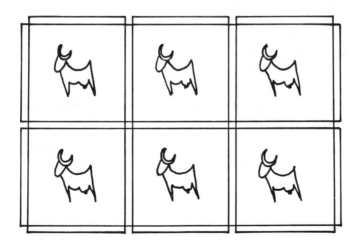

Task:

"The farmer's neighbor makes him a wager. 'If you can take away *five* gates,' he says, 'and leave *three* pens exactly the same size and shape as the ones you have now, and leave no gates lying around, then I'll buy you a dinner.' "

4. Basic Situation.
"The farmer keeps four horses too, each in a separate, square pen. For these he uses *twelve* gates."

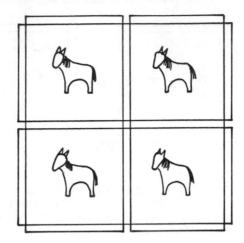

Task:
"His neighbor makes another wager. 'I'll bet you can't take *two* gates away,' he says, 'and leave *two* square pens. Just to make it easy, the two square pens don't even have to be the same size.' "

5. Basic Situation.
"By this time the neighbor is very annoyed, so he asks the farmer to put the twelve gates back into four equal squares." (as in 4)

Task:
" 'Now,' he exclaims, 'I'll bet you can't make *three* pens exactly the same size as the original by moving only *three* gates.' "

The results for each student in J-11-12 are listed below, in terms of time. That is, the length of time in minutes and seconds it took each of them to arrive at a reasonable solution within the terms of the problem*.

Sam:	Problem 1. 0:18	Rick:	Problem 1. 2:16
	2. 2:04		2. 4:21
	3. 7:16		3. 1:02
	4. 1:22		4. 1:34
	5. 4:44		5. 5:51

---

* May I suggest that you the reader, attempt these problems, time yourself, and compare your time with J-11-12.

Ashton:	Problem	1. 1:14	Angelo: Problem	1. 0:47
		2. 2:03		2. 0:13
		3. 2:43		3. 10:06
		4. 2:00		4. 5:21
		5. 1:27		5. 3:07

Jeannie:	Problem	1. 0:44	Lorne: Problem	1. 3:05
		2. 2:27		2. 4:34
		3. 2:59		3. inaccurate solution
		4. 1:44		4. inaccurate solution
		5. 3:01		5. 3:21

Freddie:	Problem	1. 2:02	Stuart: Problem	1. 1:01
		2. 2:09		2. 1:17
		3. 3:41		3. inaccurate solution
		4. 4:31		4. 3:20
		5. inaccurate solution		5. no solution

Joseph: Problem 1. 0:58
2. 1:47 — (misunderstood problem but devised
3. 5:28   a solution to the problem as he saw
4. 5:19   it.)
5. 3:10

An interesting observation, one which cannot be presented statistic- ally, or in a chart, might be of greater importance than *time* to those who are actively engaged in teaching the adolescent slower learner. None of these students gave up in defeat. This is especially significant in view of the fact that the class as a whole showed standardized test results, and general examination results that were generally very low. In other words these students were accustomed to failure, accustomed to low results and accustomed to *giving up.* Yet each of them pursued each problem to a conclusion, and achieved those conclusions with remarkable speed.

Ultimately, the willingness to think, and their tenacity, may be more important than the length of time it took each of them to solve the problems. Then too, perhaps this little experiment may be an indication that a test like the WISC is not sufficient in itself for determining the true ability of slower learning adolescents. Whatever the argument, it is fairly safe to assume that these students in J-11-12 could *think.*

CHAPTER FOURTEEN

Progress: They Have to See It!

Of the many truths one learns through the experience of teaching the adolescent slower learner, there are two which carry the ring of *absoluteness*.

1. Adolescent slower learners perform very poorly on traditional-style school examinations — that is, those examinations which are set by the school at the end of a term or semester, to evaluate students' progress in particular subjects.*

2. Yet, whenever formal examinations, or some style of school-designed formal evaluation are eliminated, there seems to develop in both teachers and students, a dangerous sense of aimlessness and indifference. A pronounced feeling that nothing is being accomplished.

Most teachers of the adolescent slower learner are caught somewhere between the two poles of this paradox: namely that examinations tend to reinforce the failure cycle, while the lack of examinations serves only to generate a sense of futility. An answer seems to lie both in a compromise and in the use of an age-old but simple, reward technique. The first is an alteration of the examining method; the second is a very ordinary progress chart.

Examining Adolescent Slower Learners in Specific Subject Areas

The slower learner's tendency to fail traditional end-of-semester examinations is the result of a combination of factors well-known to any teacher: inattention, poor communication, irregular attendance of classes, poor nutrition and health habits. But above all there is the prevailing attitude of hopelessness. Whereas the traditionally successful academic student is often excited by the challenge of an examination, and brings a sense of hope with him, the adolescent slower learner too often begins in defeat. To attack this problem and the others mentioned above, it seems logical to retreat from the traditional method somewhat, in favor of one which offers the chance of success. The key rests largely in altering the slower learner's attitude.

Instead of having them sit for semester examinations twice or three times a year, a series of short and *frequent* tests, set by individual

---

* As distinct from standardized, multiple choice, achievement tests.

teachers — not the school or a board of examiners — will provide a greater opportuntry for success.

These short tests can be structured for success, and if necessary, adjusted up or down in the scale of difficulty, according to the teacher's assessment of a class's morale. The tests can also be structured to benefit those students who have *tried*. The system need not be an escape for shirkers.

Most important, a series of short, frequent tests can provide a concrete sense of progress to students for whom success has become a long-abandoned objective. In other words, the evaluation process rather than being a mechanism for confirming ignorance and failure, can become a positive motivator.*

Structuring Classroom Tests

Over years of classroom teaching, and research with adolescent slower learners, I have come to the conclusion that when their abilities are viewed in terms of the famous Bloom Taxonomy (B. S. Bloom, et al., *Taxonomy of Educational Objectives*) they seem to function far better in the *upper* levels of the Cognitive Taxonomy, than they do in the lower. (This conclusion by the way is highly unsubstantiated by research, there being a woeful lack of it.)

Most school tests and examinations concentrate on the lower cognitive levels of the Bloom Taxonomy, namely Knowledge and Comprehension. (See reference in footnote on page 115 to the Study by Cox and Unks.) In other words, if a class of 12-13 year olds were studying the daily newspaper, a test question would likely as not read:

Give the various departments of a typical daily newspaper.

Slower learners, either because of their defeatist attitude or because they believe themselves incapable, usually have not memorized such facts and would probably fail the question. The same results would probably be obtained if a teacher of English asked:

Give a brief description of the character of "X".

Slower learners will function better on tests if two factors are considered: one, *concept* rather than content should be emphasized; two, some kind of concrete basis should appear in the question.

---

* For those who say at this point, "Ah — but in my final evaluation of students, I must still adhere to the standards set by the school", I offer this challenge: Describe precisely, in essay form, the standards set by your school (200 words or less).

Example #1

Instead of the question above, on the newspaper, the following are more likely to elicit a response, and provide an accurate assessment of how well the students understood the newspaper.

1. In what departments of the newspaper would you most likely find the following headlines? (Answer in one or two words)
   (a) Scarboro Construction Slows Down
   (b) Mortgage Rates to Increase
   (c) Arabs Attack Israel
   (d) Swiss Skier Wins Ladies' Slalom
   (e) Canada Does Not Need Medicare, Now or Ever!

2. Read carefully the following paragraph from a front page story. What "front page questions" does it answer?

   George Black, a stationary engineer at the Nielsen Co. in Don Mills, was rushed to hospital yesterday. He was overcome by fumes from a faulty gas furnace.

3. Assume that you are the news editor. Rewrite the paragraph in 2 making it *one* sentence.

4. Assume that your newspaper always supports labor unions. Which of the following three headlines would you then use over a story about a wage dispute?

   Bus Drivers Want More Money
   Bus Drivers Seek Better Wages
   Bus Drivers Threaten Strike Action

Example #2

Instead of the question calling for a brief description of someone's character, try the following:

In the story about Jo and her husband, we have come to know her rather well. Try to explain what you think Jo would do if the following things happened?

1. A clerk cheats her in a store, and she knows it.
2. Sam comes home with roses and a box of candy.
3. Jo wants to buy a coat. The salesman shows her a cherry red one, and a beige one. Which does she buy?
4. Jo is waiting for a bus on a wet day. A stranger offers her a ride in his car.
5. Jo is standing in line in front of a theatre and someone cuts in front of her, asking her if she would mind.

The fact that adolescent slower learners probably could respond quite capably to questions such as those above, does not imply that bright students are unable to function well at the higher levels of the

Bloom Taxonomy. There is no doubt that they too would perform well at these levels. It is simply that somehow the education system seems to have confused recall with achievement, and bright students are rarely challenged at the upper levels. But these students are not the subject of this book. The fact remains, in summary, that adolescent slower learners when tested briefly and frequently with instruments that use concrete situations to test concepts, will do better and will develop a sense of progress.

Designing a Progress Chart

There remains yet another weapon in the teacher's encouragement arsenal: a chart or graph maintained by each individual student. This is a visual demonstration both to the teacher and the student of the accomplishment and achievements of each member of the class. As a tool of evaluation, such a chart has little merit. But as a psychological tool, as a motivator, its merit — particularly for younger students — is unquestionable.* To a student for whom lack of achievement has become almost a way of life, a simple progress chart can be a dramatic means of reversing his failure momentum, primarily I think because it is visual and therefore immediately apparent, and secondarily, because the student makes entries and maintains the chart himself.

Interestingly the chart technique often has a positive effect on the teacher's morale as well. Although it is only a simple method of measuring (perhaps "reflecting" would be better) a student's accomplishments, it is nevertheless *concrete*. Both teacher and student develop a sense of specific accomplishment.

A Few Practical Tips

1. The chart's degree of effectiveness is usually in direct ratio to the age of the students. The younger the student, the more effective the chart becomes. Yet I have seen 18 year olds tackle their personal charts with the same eagerness as students half their age.

2. The charts should *not* be established on a competitive basis. Each student has *his own* chart; nothing is entered on it but his own accomplishments. Competition will inevitably creep in. But natural competition is considerably healthier than competition that is teacher-established.

---

* Witness the amazing success of the SRA Reading Labs (Science Research Associates, Chicago, Illinois). One of the features of these labs, a feature to which students subscribe eagerly whether or not their reading ability is helped, is the individual reading progress chart, which a student fills in as he proceeds through the scale of reading selections.

3. A chart should be designed to cover a significant period of time, a term or semester or any reasonable time block that is adaptable to the school's schedule.

4. If charts are designed to dovetail with a specific time block, it is usually effective to alter the design of the chart for the next time block (increase the value of certain accomplishments, decrease others, etc.)

The sample chart that follows is a real one. It was maintained by Ralph, a 14 year old. The time period covered was 2 months (this coincided with the school's first term).

The chart is based on units, and is designed to allow an entry on each school day. Each entry is made from the level of the previous entry. For example, if a student has amassed twelve units by September 14 (as Ralph had) and amasses no more until September 20 (as Ralph), he still maintains the level twelve, and continues to build from there.

Most students do as Ralph did, and shade in their graph right to the bottom, as they make each entry.

The units for this term were based as follows:

completed assignment in writing period	1 unit
voluntary writing assignment	5 units
solution of creative puzzle	1 unit
designed creative puzzle problem	3 units
participated in brainstorming session	1 unit
completed reading or language exercise	1 unit
read a book	5 units
joined a school club	5 units
successful in a classroom test	2 units
brought a new piece of information to class	2 units
participated in oral discussion	1 unit

(Further units available, based on other activities, but these must be negotiated with the teachers).

Note that certain activities are not listed (e.g. listening exercises) because these were not planned in the curriculum of the first term.

The objective on this particular chart was to amass 70 units by October 31. (An important feature of the chart should be that the "success level" is somewhere *below* the top of the chart.) Ralph's achievement was fairly typical; peaks and valleys, but on the whole, a

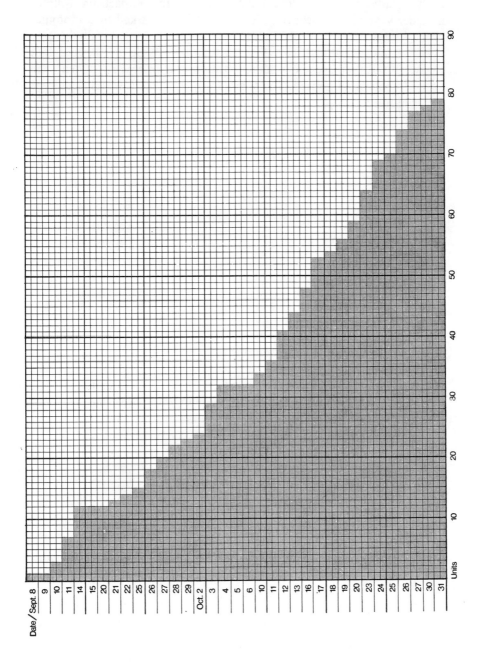

fairly steady advance. More important was the impact on Ralph's attitude. Whereas his behavior hitherto had been marked by a profound laziness, and a totally slipshod attitude to his work, he gradually became attentive and concerned. Not diligent, for miracles do not happen that easily. But Ralph became a more positive and interested student. He began to believe in himself. The chart, I am convinced, was a significant factor in this development.

CHAPTER FIFTEEN

Managing the Adolescent Slower Learner Class

Anyone who has had experience with adolescent slower learners and who makes the claim of never having had difficulty with them, is one of three things: a liar, a fool, or the school janitor.

Whether or not it is justified, adolescent slower learners have a reputation for being ill-behaved. And significantly, this reputation prevails not only among those who teach them, but as well among society at large, and particularly among the students themselves. In fact, all three groups *expect* a slower learner class to be ill-disciplined. Many teachers, therefore, shun these students, some preferring unemployment to an assignment which includes slower learner classes. Some employers and even some social agencies express quite candidly their wary attitude toward graduates of these classes. And the students, because it is the one expectation of which they can be certain, often go out of their way to fulfill it.

But They *Are* Difficult!

There is no question that adolescent slower learners are often very difficult. The wonder is however, that they behave as well as they do! How many teachers or employers would tolerate a system in which their only common experience has been failure, and in which the likelihood of continuing failure looms as an ever-constant threat? Slower learners — like anyone else — see little value in committing themselves to a system which in their experience has offered very little benefit. And one way of expressing their feelings about that system is to reject one of its vital components: standardized behavior.

Add to this the factor of culture and of class background. Many slower learners come from homes where social norms are different from those which prevail in most schools. Obedience, tact, middle-class propriety — these are not as "inbred" in the average slower learner as they are likely to be in the so-called *good* student. All too frequently, the conflict in a slower learner classroom is an outgrowth of the clash between a teacher's middle-class behavior expectations and the students' normal manner of personal conduct.

And finally there is the behavior-based natural selection that seems to take place when adolescent slower learner classes are formed. Among the members of these classes there are inevitably a few students whose personal history of disruptive behavior has led to their placement there.

Occasionally, the rationale for such placement is administrative desperation. More often it is a justified placement, inasmuch as these students have been preoccupied with mischief rather than learning. Either way, the teacher of that class is then faced with a number of experienced "disruptors" whose conduct can literally destroy the function of a whole class.

Ironically, though a teacher may be very much aware of all these factors, awareness itself is not enough to remedy the situation. And to compound the irony, there is a further problem. Despite the fact that a school system may have any number of rules, *there really are no rules of discipline.* Every teacher must deal with each class in his own way, and in the manner which best suits that class.

I Still Have To Face Them On Monday!

There may be no rules, but there are some common sense prescriptions. And by following these prescriptions, life can become considerably more pleasant for both teacher and students.

1. In the first place, firmness and a reasonable degree of structure is not misplaced in a slower learner class. Rigidity is wrong. So, ultimately, is military-style discipline. And a laissez-faire attitude from a teacher is usually the avenue to disaster. Firmness — reasonable firmness — and structure are valuable principles in classroom management because they *prevent* the majority of problems from ever occurring. Too many slower learners live in personal chaos already. They need a structure to give them guidance, a firmness against which to flex their muscles, and above all, they need the confidence, the security of knowing that in *this* classroom there are clear, reasonable expectations.

2. It follows then that for effective classroom management a teacher must be — or at least seem — organized. One more characteristic however, is equally important: a sense of humor. A teacher who takes himself too seriously unfortunately becomes an easy victim — not of the students, but of his own self-consuming passion to be perfect.

3. Preparation too, is important, for this is really an outgrowth of organization. Lack of preparation is a fairly strong guarantee of a poor lesson, and consistent failure to prepare quickly leads to the creation of a "problem class," for it is not long before students discover that once again, nothing of value is going to happen.

Regrettably, the temptation to forego preparation for a slower learner lesson is very strong. Academically trained teachers too often feel that a lesson for an unacademic class needs no preparation in depth. This kind of intellectual arrogance leads to ineffective teaching. And the next step in the sequence of events needs no description here.

4. Punishment. Usually it has only a temporary, if any, effect. To students long accustomed to punishment of various forms, one more session will make only a minimal impact. Few teachers are comfortable in meting out punishment anyway, especially if it is done privately, and punishing a student in front of his classmates is inviting defiance. Most students who need a reminder of some kind can be effectively approached on a private, personal basis. There are few students who will not yield to common sense in a mature, sincere discussion of their "problem."

5. The "bad" class. Thinking about their one "bad" class causes some teachers to lose sleep at night. All their teaching successes are overshadowed by the cloud of feelings about this one group. Few teachers can define precisely what makes this class "bad", but once this feeling prevails, once this reputation is established, a barrier comes down between teacher and students.

    In my teaching career I have encountered defiance, indifference, rebellion; I have dealt with countless incomplete assignments, and once even changed the diaper — in class — on the illegitimate son of one of my students, but I have *never* met a class that is all bad. This is a particularly important point for young teachers who are on the brink of resignation. The vast majority of so-called bad classes have garnered their reputation through the machinations of a few specific students. These few must be recognized and dealt with — the earlier the better — and management of the "bad class" becomes a much simpler task.

6. Some small practical tips.
    (a) If a class tends to be boisterous, or difficult to control — particularly on certain days of the week or certain days of the year — design some individualized work for them. Structure the situation so that each student will work by himself in the classroom. However, this planning will be next to useless unless the teacher circulates around the class giving individual help and encouragement, or perhaps just chatting with certain students. The reason for this technique is to establish an atmosphere of calm and stability in the class. At the same time it gives

a perceptive teacher an opportunity to establish an individual rapport with many students in the group, a rapport that hopefully is built on mutual respect. These individual relationships will make whole-class lessons more effective, and will help establish a positive attitude. Very often then, those individuals who refuse to cooperate, are controlled by peer group pressure.

(b) A device as simple as the seating arrangement of the class may be the key to effective management. Place individual students so that the dynamic of their personalities is either developed or if necessary, curbed. Most disruptive students need a foil or an audience. Compulsive extroverts need to be highly visible. Seat these people accordingly; they are less tempted to perform without an audience.

(c) Keep extra materials, pens, pencils, etc., in the classroom. Live with the fact that slower learners inevitably *forget*. (And try to discover too, *why* they always forget; it could be the teacher.)

(d) Realize that slower learners are probably going to be noisier, more restive, and less diligent than many of their more successful colleagues. Learn to live with this.

(e) The first day and the first week are vital. In fact they can determine the course of the year.

In the final analysis, classroom management is really a personal matter between the teacher and his adolescent slower learner class. What upsets one teacher or one class, may not affect another. To some people, classroom management means absolute silence; to others it means "anything goes" as long as learning takes place.

Whatever one's interpretation of management may be, the ultimate judgment is whether or not the students gain cognitively, perceptively, intellectually, emotionally. For the teacher who cares, who tries, and who recognizes and attempts to meet the real needs of his students, management problems soon disappear. To this person, teaching the adolescent slower learner is an exciting challenge in which the drawbacks and discomforts are far outweighed by the rewards.

Bibliography

Early in my undergraduate years at university, I was led to a few observations about the huge, multi-paged bibliographies that are usually distributed to students at the beginning of a course. In the first place, their size effectively eliminated any hope in the average student of ever achieving a level of expertise in the subject. As a consequence, these thick bundles of paper tended to be used as fire-starters, or in some cases, as wedges to build up uneven table legs. For other students, these bibliographies tended to settle, like sediment, to the bottom of every pile of unused and forgotten lecture notes. Hence I decided that if ever I were in a position to distribute bibliographies, they would always be pertinent but brief and would be submitted twice yearly to rigorous surgery.

Because of my second promise, this bibliography is presented reluctantly, for surely by the time this book is printed, at least one new significant work will appear which no doubt should replace a title already included.

However, each title in this brief list can be very helpful to anyone concerned with the adolescent slower learner. Furthermore, each title contains within itself, bibliographic material for those who wish to pursue a subject further. Thus with some optimism, and not a little apprehension, I present the following list — realizing as always, that no book of theory or practice is of any avail without a teacher whose primary motivations are genuine concern and common sense.

The following titles are "*must*-reading". They should be in the personal library of all teachers of the adolescent slower learner.

1. Beard, R.M. *An Outline of Piaget's Developmental Psychology*.
   London: Routledge & Kegan Paul, 1969.

2. Bruner, J., et al. *Studies In Cognitive Growth*.
   New York: John Wiley & Sons, 1966.

3. Creber, J. W. P. *Lost For Words*.
   Middlesex, England: Penguin Books, 1972.

4. Dixon, John. *Growth Through English*.
   National Association For the Teaching of English, 1967.

5. Fader, D. N. and McNeil, E. B., *Hooked on Books*.
   New York: Berkley Publishing Corp., 1968.

6. Herriot, P. *Language & Teaching: A Psychological View*.
   London: Routledge and Kegan Paul, 1968.

7. Holbrook, D. *English For the Rejected*.
   Cambridge: Cambridge University Press, 1965.

8. Lawton, D. *Social Class, Language And Education*.
   London: Routledge and Kegan Paul, 1968.

9. Stott, D. H. *Studies of Troublesome Children*.
   London: Tavistock Publications, 1966.

Of the many surveys on slower learners, on class structure etc., the following seem to be most immediately useful for teachers of the adolescent slower learner.

1. Bernstein, B. "Social Structure, Language and Learning".
   Education Research, number 3, 1961.
2. Goldfarb, W. "Infant Rearing and Problem Behavior".
   American Journal of Orthopsychiatry, number 13, 1943.
3. Goldfarb, W. "The Effects of Early Institutional Care on Adolescent Personality".
   Journal of Experimental Education, number 12, 1943.
4. Kaufman, S. "Issues In Evaluating Occupational Programmes".
   Toronto Board of Education, number 101, 1971.
5. Miller, G. W. "Factors In School Achievement and Social Class".
   Journal of Education Psychology, number 61, 1970.
6. Reich, C. M. and Zeigler, S., "A Follow-Up Study of Special Vocational and Special High School Students".
   Toronto Board of Education, 1970.
7. Wright, E. N. *Student's Background And Its Relationship To Class And Program In School.*
   Toronto Board of Education, 1970.

Each of the following have merit of one kind or another, especially in helping teachers develop curriculum for the adolescent slower learner.

1. Abrahams, R. D., and Troike, R. C. *Language and Cultural Diversity In American Education.*
   New Jersey: Prentice-Hall, 1972.
2. Blackwell, R. B., & Joynt, R. R. *Learning Disabilities Handbook For Teachers.*
   Springfield: Charles C. Thomas, 1972.
3. Brown, R. I., ed. *The Assessment and Education of Slow-Learning Children.*
   London: University of London Press, 1967.
4. Cayer, R. L., et al. *Listening and Speaking.*
   New York: Collier-Macmillan, 1971.
5. Fagan, E. R. *English And The Disadvantaged.*
   Scranton, Pennsylvania: Intext Publishing Company, 1967.
6. Furneaux, B. *The Special Child.*
   Middlesex: Penguin Books, 1969.
7. Gaddis, E. A. *Teaching The Slower Learner In The Regular Classroom.*
   Belmont, California: Fearon Publishers, 1971.
8. Hoffman, B. *The Tyranny of Testing.*
   New York: Crowell-Collier-Macmillan Inc., 1962.
9. Kephart, N. C. *The Slow Learner In the Classroom,* 2nd ed.
   Columbus, Ohio: Charles E. Merrill, 1971.

10. Tansley, A. E. and Gulliford, R. *The Education of Slow Learning Children.*
    London: Routledge and Kegan Paul, 1960.

11. Wilkinson, A. *The Foundations of Language.*
    London: Oxford Press, 1971.

12. Wilkinson, A. "Spoken English".
    Occasional Publications #2, University of Birmingham.
    (available through Oxford Press)

Acknowledgments

I Taught Them All by Naomi John White, p. 28. Reprinted by permission from *The Clearing House,* vol. 12, no. 3 (November, 1937).

Why Has the Population Problem Become a Crisis? p. 54. Reprinted by permission from *The Population Bomb* by Paul R. Ehrlich. Original copyright 1968 by Paul R. Ehrlich. Revised and expanded edition, 1971. Published by Ballantine Books, Inc.

NASA Moon Survival Task, p. 55. Permission to reprint granted by the author, Joy Hall, Ph.D., and publisher, Teleometrics International, Copyright 1963.

Food Raids by Brazil Peasants, p. 65. Reprinted by permission of Reuters.

Ghostly Furniture-Moving Force Hangs Over Boy, 11, p. 68. Reprinted by permission of The Toronto Sun.

Face Names, p. 85; **Names, Please,** p. 89. Reprinted by permission from *4th Junior Puzzle Book* by N. G. Pulsford (London: Pan, 1958).

Why We Split Up, p. 97. Reprinted from *Chatelaine* (July, 1969) by permission of *Chatelaine Magazine.*

Skier to Take on Everest, p. 102. Reprinted by permission of Reuters.

The Diary of Anne Frank (May 3, 1944), p. 103. Reprinted from *The Diary of Anne Frank* by permission of Doubleday & Co. Inc., New York, and Vallentine, Mitchell & Co., Ltd., London.

The author wishes to acknowledge the research work and data collection, as well as the verification of data and proof-reading done by Rita Weber.